FABIAN
LIBERTARIANISM

FABIAN LIBERTARIANISM

100 Years to Freedom

Martin Cowen

Copyright © 2016 by Martin Cowen.
Author of Fellowship of Reason: A Moral Community for the 21st Century

Library of Congress Control Number: 2016906456
ISBN: Hardcover   978-1-5144-8690-0
          Softcover   978-1-5144-8689-4
          eBook   978-1-5144-8688-7

All rights reserved. No part of this book may be reproduced or transmitted in any form or by any means, electronic or mechanical, including photocopying, recording, or by any information storage and retrieval system, without permission in writing from the copyright owner.

Any people depicted in stock imagery provided by Thinkstock are models, and such images are being used for illustrative purposes only.
Certain stock imagery © Thinkstock.

Print information available on the last page.

Rev. date: 04/25/2016

To order additional copies of this book, contact:
Xlibris
1-888-795-4274
www.Xlibris.com
Orders@Xlibris.com
733407

CONTENTS

Introduction xiii
    Fabian Libertarianism xiii
    Quintus Fabius Maximus Cunctator xvi
    One hundred Years to Freedom xvii
    Freedom xviii
    Conclusion xix

Chapter 1—Leviathan 1
    Leviathan Is Evil 1
    Leviathan Is the Cause of Our Societal Problems 4
    Leviathans Separate Existence 4
    Life Span 5
    The Organs of Superorganisms 6
        Propaganda (Communication of Mission) 6
        Information Filter 7
            Internal Information 7
            Information Coming into or Going Out of the
                Superorganism 9
            Human Resources (HR) 12
            Self-defense 14
    Leviathan Big Government 15
    Leviathan Need Not Be Governmental 17
    Conclusion 18

Chapter 2—Leviathan Education 20
    The Key to Utopia: Government Education 20
    Sociopathic Leviathan 21
    Leviathan's Mission 22
    Why Is Leviathan Wicked? 24
    Who Works for Leviathan? 26
        Innocents 26
        Time markers 26

>   Stars 27
>   Innovators 28
>   Slugs 29
>   Sociopaths 30
> Conclusion 31

Chapter 3—Economics 33
  The Simple Rules of Economics 33
    Rule 1 33
    Rule 2 33
      Demand-Price Example 34
      Supply-Price Example 34
  Minimum Wage 35
    Wages Are Prices 35
    Retired Lady Example 36
    Unpaid College Intern 36
    Unemployed Young Adult 37
    Leviathan's Strawman 37
    Consequences of the Minimum Wage 38
    Libertarians Are Not Luddites 40
    The Total Cost of Labor 40
    Conclusion on the Minimum Wage 41
  Household Servants 41
  Healthcare 42
    Tinkering with Demand 43
    Tinkering with Price 44
    Tinkering with Supply 45
      Professional Licensing 45
      Medical Care in the Absence of Licensing 46
    Self-Help Medicine 47
  Free-Market Health Insurance 48
    World War II Origin 48
    Routine Services Are Not Insurable 48
    Imminent Risks Are Not Insurable 49
  Repealing Obamacare 50
  Demand for Great Doctors 50
  Doctoring: An Honorable Profession 51

  The Great Recession/Depression 52
   The Cause of Recessions 52
    A Local Depression 52
    China's Coming Depression 53
    Subsidizing Depressions 53
    Unfunded Government Pensions 54
  Leviathan's Cost Interventions 55
  American Oligarchy 56
  Plato's Cave; Neo's Red Pill 57
  Conclusion on Economics 58

Chapter 4—The Little People 60
  The Three Languages of Politics 60
  "The Little People" Need . . . Whatever 61
  Especially Needy People Do Exist 62
  Progressives and Conservatives Believe Themselves
   "Superior" 63
  The "It's Force" Argument 63
  The Water Fountain Metaphor 64
  The Individual as Moral Center of the Universe 65
  Progressive and Conservatives Are Not Gods 66
  Leviathan Creates "The Little People" 67
  Conclusion 68

Chapter 5—Whose Question Is It? 69
  The Great Leap Forward 70
  Scientism 71
  Little "o" objectivists 72
  Why Are We Inclined to Meddle? 73
   24/7 News Media 73
   No Privacy 73
  Mind Your Own Business 74
   Natural Law 74
   The Frog and the Boiling Pot 75
   Freedom Is Not the Right to Vote 76
  Review the Questions 76
  Conclusion 78

Chapter 6—The Plan: Act One 80
Look to Our Own Moral Characters 81
Courage 82
Temperance 85
Generosity 85
Magnificence 86
Magnanimity 87
Appetite for Honor 88
Gentleness 88
Truthfulness 89
Charm 90
Friendliness 90
Sense of Shame 90
Righteous Indignation 91
Justice 91
Conclusion of Act One 93

Chapter 7—The Plan: Act Two 94
Learn the Rules 94
Local Sign Ordinance 95
Candidate Qualifications 96
Lobbyist Defined 96
Use of State Seal 99
Many More Laws 100
Political Offices 100
Not Fabian Target Offices 100
The Sheriff's Office 101
The Probate Court 101
The Water Authority 102
The Board of Education 102
United States Congress 103
Fabian Target Offices 103
The Board of County Commissioners 103
State Legislature 104
Conclusion of Act Two 105

Chapter 8—The Plan: Act Three 107
   Avoid the Enemy 107
      Soft Targets 108
         The Incumbent 108
         The District 109
         The Fabian Libertarian Candidate 109
         Special Statewide Support 109
      The Aftermath 110
   Targeting Thugs 110
   Education 112
      The Luddite Fallacy 113
      Privacy 117
   Conclusion to Act Three 123

Chapter 9—No Federal Taxes 124
   The Presidency 127
   The Congress 127
   The Federal Courts 128
   Federal Police 129
   The Alphabet Soup of Federal Agencies 129
   The Military 129
   Conclusion 132

Chapter 10—Leave No Trace Behind 133
   Communist Countries 134
   Privatize Public Property 135
   Freedom and Responsibility 135
   Examples 137
   Land Viewed as "Commons" 139
   Conclusion to "Leave No Trace Behind" 140

Chapter 11—Abortion 141
   Cover for Leviathan 141
   Scratch a Zealot and Find a Sinner 143
      The Pro-*Choice* Zealot 143

    The Pro-*Life* Zealot 144
        Atonement 144
        Anthropomorphization 144
        Children Are Sacred 145
    Summarizing the Emotional Issues 146
  The Politics of Abortion 147
  The Ethics of Abortion 148
    Two Ethical Examples at the Extremes 150
        Case One 150
        Case Two 152
        The Astonishing Presumption of Pro-lifers 153
  Conclusion on Abortion 153

Chapter 12—Conclusion 154
  One Hundred Years: Not So Long a Time 154
  The Great Depression II 155
  The Invention of Freedom 157
    The City-State 158
    Are Not We All on Pharaoh's Leash? 160
    Movement as the Cause of Freedom 161
    Freedom as an Act of the Will 162
  The End 164

Bibliography 165

Dedicated to our beautiful sons, Lindsey, who is autistic and especially needy, and Alexander, who is especially capable and who, after their parents are gone, will care for his beloved brother for as long as they both shall live.

Introduction

This introduction explains our title, *Fabian Libertarianism: 100 Years to Freedom*. First, we examine Fabian Libertarianism. Next, we introduce Quintus Fabius Maximus Cunctator. Then, we discuss why freedom will take one hundred years to recover. Finally, freedom is defined.

Fabian Libertarianism

The name *Fabian Libertarianism* is an allusion to the Fabian Society, a British Socialist think tank. While Libertarianism and Socialism are philosophical opposites, Libertarians have a lot to learn from the Fabian Society.

The Fabian Society was founded on January 4, 1884, exactly 132 years from the writing of these words. The society was named after Fabius Maximus (280–203 BC), the great Roman general. His agnomen, *Cunctator*, is related to the obsolete English word *cunctation*, which means delay. "For the right moment you must wait, as Fabius did most patiently, when warring against Hannibal, though many censured his delays; but when the time comes you must strike hard, as Fabius did, or your waiting will be in vain, and fruitless."[1]

George Bernard Shaw (1856–1950), Nobel Prize–winning Irish playwright, and H.G. Wells (1866–1946), English novelist (e.g., *The Time Machine*, *The Invisible Man*, and *The War of the Worlds*), are famous Fabian Socialists.

Among the many essays written by Fabian Socialists are these, giving an idea of what the Fabian Society advocated:

- Why are the Many Poor? (1884, W. L. Phillips)
- A Manifesto (1884, G. Bernard Shaw)

- Practical Land Nationalisation (1890, Sidney Webb)
- A Plea for Eight Hours Bill (1890, Sidney Webb)
- The Municipalisation of the Gas Supply (1891, Sidney Webb)
- Christian Socialism (1892, Rev. Stewart D. Headlam)
- The Unemployed (1893, John Burns)
- The Case for State Pensions in Old Age (1896, George Turner)
- Houses for the People (1897, Arthur Hickmott)
- Municipal Water (1897, C. M. Knowles)
- The Workmen's Compensation Act (1897, C. R. Allen, Jr.)
- State Arbitration and the Living Wage (1897, H. W. Macrosty)
- Liquor Licensing at Home and Abroad (1897, Edward R. Pease)
- The Municipalisation of the Milk Supply (1899, Dr. G. F. McCleary)
- Municipal Hospitals (1900)
- Municipal Fire Insurance (1990, Mrs. Fenton MacPherson)
- Municipal Steamboats (1900, S. D. Shallard)
- State Railways for Ireland (1900, Clement Edwards, MP)
- The Education Muddle and the Way Out (1901, Sidney Webb)
- Socialism for Millionaires (1901, Bernard Shaw)
- State Aid to Agriculture (1903, T. S. Dymond)
- Public Control of Electric Power and Transit (1905, S. G. Hobson)
- The Case for a Legal Minimum Wage (1906, W. Stephen Sanders)
- The Case for School Nurseries (1909, Mrs. Townshend)
- The Endowment of Motherhood (1910, Henry D. Harben)
- A National Medical Service (1911, L. Lawson Dodd)
- The Economic Foundations of the Women's Movement (1914, Mabel Atkinson)
- War and the Workers: Handbook of some immediate measures to present Unemployment and relieve distress (1914, Sidney Webb)

The amazing fact is that the Fabian Society has accomplished all of its goals. "We are all Socialists now."[2]

In light of this list of Fabian Society essays, consider these modern American facts:

FABIAN LIBERTARIANISM

- The United States Federal Government owns 84 percent of Nevada and 28 percent of all land in America.
- The legal workweek is forty hours.
- Natural gas is a tightly controlled government monopoly.
- Unemployment is subsidized by the government (unemployment insurance).
- Social Security funds old age and disability.
- Public and subsidized housing is widespread.
- Water service is provided by most municipal governments.
- All states have worker's compensation laws.
- The "living wage" is currently a hot topic.
- Liquor is licensed ubiquitously.
- The milk industry is highly regulated, and the sale of raw milk is illegal in most places.
- There are many public hospitals.
- The insurance industry is tightly regulated.
- Public transportations, including ferryboats like the Staten Island Ferry, are everywhere.
- Amtrak is the government-subsidized national passenger railway.
- Education is nationalized, except for a few who escape to private schools and homeschooling.
- Many prominent Socialists are millionaires.
- Agriculture is subsidized by the government.
- There is a national minimum wage. In some jurisdictions, the minimum wages is as high as $15 per hour.
- There are public kindergartens and subsidized daycare for children.
- Motherhood (and now fatherhood) is subsidized by government-mandated programs like parental leave.
- Healthcare is effectively nationalized.

"The barbarians have breached the walls of the city. The city is sacked and ravaged. All the men are killed. The women and children are sold into slavery." (Anonymous.)

Most Americans do not even regard any of the above-listed Socialist programs as a problem.

MARTIN COWEN

Quintus Fabius Maximus Cunctator

Quintus Fabius Maximus Cunctator (275–203 BC) was a Roman consul five times. He was twice dictator. As consul and dictator, he commanded the Roman army at various times during the Second Punic War (218–201 BC). The major event of the war is the invasion of Italy by the Carthaginian general Hannibal. The famous Greek historian Plutarch (46–127) and his *Life of Fabius Maximus* is the source for the information about Fabius in this introduction. Roman historian Livy (64 BC–AD 17) and the Greek historian Polybius (200–118 BC) are valuable sources also.

Hannibal ravaged Italy from north to south from 218 to 203 BC. The suffering was enormous. After the Battle of Trebia (218 BC) and the Battle at Lake Trasimene (217 BC), Fabius, aged fifty-eight and held in high esteem by the Roman people, was appointed prodictator. Upon his appointment, Fabius turned Rome's attention to religious rites, which Fabius thought had been neglected.

In military matters, according to Plutarch, Fabius' "tactics were slow, silent, and yet relentless in their steady pressure, [Hannibal's] strength was gradually and imperceptibly undermined and drained away.[3]

As might be suspected, Fabius' delaying tactics against Hannibal were not at first appreciated by the Roman people who wanted action. Fabius' prodictatorship expired at the end of 217 BC. The people of Rome were frustrated with Fabius' delaying tactics and lack of action. Terentius Varro and Paulus Aemilius were appointed coconsuls for 216 BC. The consuls divided the command of the Roman army, each consul taking command on alternate days. General Hannibal and Consul Varro, both of whom were anxious for battle, met at Cannae, a city on the Adriatic Sea near the "heel" of the boot that is the geographical shape of Italy. The Roman army was twice the size of the Carthaginian army at this place.

The tactics of the Battle of Cannae (August 2, 216 BC) are famous and are taught in military academies worldwide. Rome lost. Plutarch reports that fifty thousand Romans were killed. Polybius reports the death of seventy thousand. Livy reports forty thousand infantry slain. Perhaps one in four Romans of fighting age died at the Battle of Cannae, the greatest ever defeat in battle for Rome. Consul Paulus

Aemilius died in the battle. The rash Consul Terentius Varro escaped and returned to Rome.

The Roman people turned again to Fabius for leadership. Fabius served as consul in 215 (the year following the Battle of Cannae), 214, and 209 BC. Fabius' agnomen *Cunctator* (Delayer), once a term of opprobrium, was now his badge of honor. Fabius' delaying tactics now seemed like acts of genius following the disaster at Cannae.

As of this writing American Freedom has lost its Battle of Cannae to the Socialists. From this defeat American Freedom will recover in time.

One hundred Years to Freedom

One hundred years seems like a long time. For many Americans, especially young Americans, there is little difference between an event occurring one hundred years ago and one occurring four hundred years ago. Both are ancient history. Almost one hundred years ago (April 6, 1917), America declared war on Germany in the middle of World War I. Four hundred years ago, William Shakespeare (1564–1616) and Miguel de Cervantes (1546–1616), author of *Don Quixote*, both died on April 23, 1616. Both World War I and the death of two of the world's greatest writers are either ancient history or completely unknown to a majority of Americans. Even the Vietnam War (1955–1975) is ancient history to many, having occurred before the birth of over one-half of living Americans.

Planning, for many of us, is for the weekend. Now, that is long range! Planning for retirement is mostly left to the government or to our employers. Parents have children and are obliged to raise them for twenty-plus years. Some parents, we suppose, do a little planning for their children. But who among us plans for one hundred years?

Yeoman farmers (farmers who work their own land) understand planning for decades, if not for a century or centuries. The author had his first inkling of a difference in perspective between farmers and the rest of us when he encountered a seventy-year-old French-immigrant pecan farmer in middle Georgia decades ago. The Frenchman was planting new pecan trees on his land. Pecan trees can take up to ten years to produce nuts. It was doubtful that the septuagenarian would ever see any nuts from his newly planted trees.

Victor Davis Hanson, himself a yeoman farmer, in his book *The Other Greeks: The Family Farm and the Agrarian Roots of Western Civilization*, makes clear the role of the yeoman farmer in the creation of the values that are the foundation of America. In ancient Greece, according to Hanson, the yeoman was farmer, citizen, and soldier. The yeoman's virtues of productivity, independence, and courage are the foundations of American Freedom.

The family farmer is often farming land that his father, grandfather, and great-grandfather owned. He plans to pass on his farm to his children and grandchildren. In this context, a seventy-year-old man planting pecan trees that will not bear fruit until he is eighty years old is completely understandable. Five or six generations on one family farm equals 150 or 180 years of work and long-range planning.

The author is almost sixty-five years old upon the publication of this book. The Libertarian Party, founded on December 11, 1971, is forty-five years old. The author believes (no Internet record of the event to verify the date or event title) he attended the first convention of the Georgia Libertarian Party in 1972 at the Americana Hotel on Peachtree Street in Atlanta, Georgia, at age twenty-two. Older Americans can see most of the arc of one hundred years. The task of older Americans is to teach young Americans that the arc exists.

The Fabian Society, as indicated above, has achieved a complete victory over American Freedom. Their victory comes 132 years after their founding in 1884. To reverse this disaster will take another 100 years.

Freedom

What is freedom? Freedom is the protection of property rights by the rule of law. Yes, it is that simple. Property rights include the rights to life, liberty, the pursuit of happiness, and private personal property. Property rights, as used in this book, also include the so-called Civil Rights stated in the Bill of Rights to the U.S. Constitution, such as freedom of speech, freedom of religion, freedom of association, the right to bear arms, and so on.

Freedom is not the right to vote, which is what most Americans think. The right to vote is simply one of several constitutional tools designed to protect property rights.

America was founded based upon the values of the Enlightenment. Enlightenment thinkers like John Locke (1632–1704) and Adam Smith (1723–1790) greatly influenced our founding fathers.

Adam Smith said, "It is not from the benevolence of the butcher, the brewer, or the baker that we expect our dinner, but from their regard to their own interests." John Locke said, "Every man has a property in his own person. This nobody has a right to, but himself." John Locke also said, "Government has no other end, but the preservation of property."

The values of the Enlightenment were well established in America by the time of our 1776 American Revolution. (The Declaration of Independence was proclaimed and published on July 4, 1776.) The values that have destroyed American Freedom come from French philosopher Jean-Jacques Rousseau (1712–1778), among others. Rousseau's ideas were expressed in the French Revolution that began with the storming of the Bastille on July 14, 1789. Rousseau expressed the view that property rights were merely a social construct. He also advocated the notion of the General Will. A citizen's **acceptance** of the General Will *is* freedom according to Rousseau. These two ideas are now fully absorbed in America and are the reason that American Freedom has collapsed into socialism. It has taken two-hundred-plus years (1789 to 2016) for Americans to embrace the ideas of the Father of Democratic Totalitarianism, Jean-Jacques Rousseau.

Rousseau's idea that we are all willing participants in a "social contract" allows modern Americans to believe that whatever is the product of voting is a legitimate exercise of authority, no matter what property rights are violated.

Conclusion

To conclude this introduction, we have explained that "Fabian Libertarianism" is an allusion to the Socialist Fabian Society, founded in 1884 and still existing today. "Fabian" is an adjectival allusion to Fabius Maximus, the famous Roman general who opposed Hannibal in the Second Punic War. "One Hundred Years to Freedom" suggests that the plan, detailed in this book, to restore American Freedom will take a long time to execute. Finally, we have asserted and shown that "freedom" is not simply, as most Americans believe, the right to vote. Freedom is the protection of property rights by the rule of law.

There is hope to recover American Freedom for our children and grandchildren. We need to take the long view, create a plan, execute the plan with gradualism and persistence, and take pride in the fact that we are doing Good Works for people that matter to us, ourselves, our children, and our fellow citizens. Now, let us state our **one-hundred-years plan** to restore American Freedom.

Chapter 1—Leviathan

The goal of this chapter is to persuade the reader that there is something very wrong in the political world. The cause of the political malfunction is what we shall call Leviathan.

Superorganisms exist. They consist of individual human beings. Superorganisms have lives separate from the individual human beings of which they are composed. Superorganisms are epiphenomena of human social groups. Examples of superorganisms include government bureaucracies like the United States Department of Veterans Affairs (VA), unions like the National Education Association (NEA), and corporations like General Electric (GE). In this book, the name *Leviathan* is given to these superorganisms. Leviathan, as we will see, is a deadly enemy.

Leviathan Is Evil

Superorganisms are groups of human beings. Like all living beings, superorganisms seek to live. Human beings seek to live, but they seek the *good* life through the creation of lasting values and through procreation, children. Since superorganisms are eternal, they do not need to procreate in order to continue their existence. They seek only more life. **Superorganisms do not seek the good life**.

The *good* life for human beings is a flourishing life. In the Fellowship of Reason (FOR), a Georgia nonprofit moral community, the flourishing life is expressed by the Greek term *eudaimonia*, or well-being-ism. Just as a pecan tree flourishes or not, so too a human being flourishes or not. A flourishing pecan tree is large, well-formed, verdant green in season, and productive of sweet, savory nuts. A nonflourishing pecan tree is puny, malformed, diseased, and barren. A flourishing human being is well-formed, robustly healthy, happy in her work and family with a spouse and healthy children. A nonflourishing human being is alone, diseased, emaciated, shivering next to an urban heating vent barely covered by an old newspaper. A human being seeks to flourish because she is self-conscious and desires the mental condition we call happiness. ***Morality is that set of rules that allows human beings to flourish. The moral virtues include courage, moderation, generosity, magnificence, magnanimity, pride, truthfulness, wittiness, friendliness, righteous indignation, justice, independence, and productivity.***

Morality and virtue mean nothing to Leviathan. Leviathan is not self-conscious. Leviathan is like poison ivy that moves in response to stimuli from the environment. Good movements are those which allow the vine to live and grow. Bad movements are those that result in injury and death. Poison ivy, like Leviathan, has no goal other than life and more life. Because Leviathan does not seek the ***good*** life; Leviathan does not need morality. Leviathan is amoral. Leviathan is inimical to human morality.

Because Leviathan is composed of and served by human beings, the human beings must be persuaded that they are enabling and serving a ***good*** cause, a cause that advances the ***good*** life, a cause that is ***moral***. Therefore, Leviathan has a cover story, a rationale for its existence. The VA exists to serve the needs of veterans and their families. The NEA exists "to advocate for education professionals and to unite our members and the nation to fulfill the promise of public education to prepare every student to succeed in a diverse and interdependent world." GE exists to imagine, build, solve, and lead. Leviathan's ***reason*** for being (as opposed to its rationale) is life and more life, ***without regard to morality.***

Consider the following description of Leviathan from the Book of Job in the Old Testament (King James Version):

Job 41:1–34:

1. Canst thou draw out leviathan with a hook? or his tongue with a cord which thou lettest down?
2. Canst thou put an hook into his nose? or bore his jaw through with a thorn?
3. Will he make many supplications unto thee? will he speak soft words unto thee?

4. Will he make a covenant with thee? wilt thou take him for a servant for ever?
5. Wilt thou play with him as with a bird? or wilt thou bind him for thy maidens?
6. Shall the companions make a banquet of him? shall they part him among the merchants?
7. Canst thou fill his skin with barbed irons? or his head with fish spears?
8. Lay thine hand upon him, remember the battle, do no more.
9. Behold, the hope of him is in vain: shall not one be cast down even at the sight of him?
10. None is so fierce that dare stir him up: who then is able to stand before me?
11. Who hath prevented me, that I should repay him? whatsoever is under the whole heaven is mine.
12. I will not conceal his parts, nor his power, nor his comely proportion.
13. Who can discover the face of his garment? or who can come to him with his double bridle?
14. Who can open the doors of his face? his teeth are terrible round about.
15. His scales are his pride, shut up together as with a close seal.
16. One is so near to another, that no air can come between them.
17. They are joined one to another, they stick together, that they cannot be sundered.
18. By his neesings a light doth shine, and his eyes are like the eyelids of the morning.
19. Out of his mouth go burning lamps, and sparks of fire leap out.
20. Out of his nostrils goeth smoke, as out of a seething pot or caldron.
21. His breath kindleth coals, and a flame goeth out of his mouth.
22. In his neck remaineth strength, and sorrow is turned into joy before him.
23. The flakes of his flesh are joined together: they are firm in themselves; they cannot be moved.
24. His heart is as firm as a stone; yea, as hard as a piece of the nether millstone.

25. When he raiseth up himself, the mighty are afraid: by reason of breakings they purify themselves.
26. The sword of him that layeth at him cannot hold: the spear, the dart, nor the habergeon.
27. He esteemeth iron as straw, and brass as rotten wood.
28. The arrow cannot make him flee: slingstones are turned with him into stubble.
29. Darts are counted as stubble: he laugheth at the shaking of a spear.
30. Sharp stones are under him: he spreadeth sharp pointed things upon the mire.
31. He maketh the deep to boil like a pot: he maketh the sea like a pot of ointment.
32. He maketh a path to shine after him; one would think the deep to be hoary.
33. Upon earth there is not his like, who is made without fear.
34. He beholdeth all high things: he is a king over all the children of pride.

Leviathan Is the Cause of Our Societal Problems

Our goal is to explain how it is that so many societal problems are intractable. For example, how is it that Thomas Edison's great invention, the incandescent light bulb, is outlawed in America? How is it that veterans beloved of Americans are denied treatment by the U.S. Department of Veterans Affairs (VA) unto death? How is it that bad teachers are kept on indefinitely by a school system at full pay in isolated Temporary Reassignment Centers ("rubber rooms")[4] in New York City? ***The heretofore undiscovered answer is: superorganisms having ultimate power over us.***

Leviathans Separate Existence

The concept of independent corporate existence is easy. Consider, for example, the Fellowship of Reason in ethical living and continuing adult education, is one of many moral communities.[5] FOR has by-laws, acts through a board of trustees, and is nonpolitical. No single member, not even the president, can speak for the corporation. Only the board of trustees, as a board, acting by majority vote, speaks for the corporation. FOR is a different entity from its individual members, defined by its by-laws and activity through its board of trustees. Simple.

Size matters. When an organization reaches a certain size, an epiphenomenon occurs. A superorganism comes into existence.

By the end of this chapter, we will see that our society is controlled by a number of interacting superorganisms whose existence, heretofore unknown, is a threat to **human morality**. Science fiction anticipates that artificial intelligence (AI) will be deadly for the existence of human beings. However, **human morality** is already significantly compromised by Leviathan.

Let us consider Leviathan.

Life Span

Leviathan lives forever. General Electric (GE) was founded in 1892 by Thomas Edison (1847–1931). In 1776, the Continental Congress started providing benefits for disabled soldiers. Now we have the VA. The National Education Associate (NEA) was founded in 1857. These superorganisms will never die as long as America exists. Superorganisms are eternal.

An individual might live for seventy years. "The days of our years are three-score years and ten; and if by reason of strength *they be* fourscore years, yet *is* their strength labour and sorrow, for it is soon cut off, and we fly away" (Psalms 90:10). The active adult portion of a human life endures for fifty years, if we are lucky. Our political lives, if existing at all, might last for a few years of vain tilting at windmills. Immortal Leviathan, who "esteemeth iron as straw, *and* brass as rotten wood" and who "laugheth at the shaking of a spear" is completely disinterested in the isolated human beings. The individual's political life span is infinitesimal compared to the eternal life of Leviathan. The individual human being to Leviathan is like an ant to a man.

A corollary to its immortal life is the scope of Leviathan's action. Leviathan acts over decades and centuries. Yeoman farmers (small family farmers who work their own land) act over decades, but these days few Americans are yeoman farmers. In the introduction, we told the story of the seventy-year-old French tree farmer planting pecan trees not expected to reach full nut production for ten years. The yeoman farmer thinks of his descendants who will inherit the family farm.

City folk, the majority of us, act not over a range of decades and certainly not with centuries in mind. Some city folk save for retirement (a decades-long project), but what else do we do that involves acting toward a goal one or several decades hence? Children come to mind. We have our children for at least twenty years while they mature. Some parents plan for those years, especially for college. Responsible parents cannot do otherwise. How can we city folk hope to act against Leviathan who plans for decades and centuries, when we city folk merely plan for the weekend?

Individuals, especially live-for-the-moment city folk, are no match for immortal Leviathan. City folk are not even aware of the enemy. People are blind to immortal Leviathan who rules us.

The Organs of Superorganisms

"Canst thou draw out leviathan with an hook? or his tongue with a cord *which* thou lettest down?" (Job 41:1).

Leviathan is composed of human beings. Individuals are the cells of the superorganism. Like biological organisms, superorganisms have organs. The cells (human beings) form the organs within the superorganism. The organs have specialized functions.

Propaganda (Communication of Mission)

One organ of Leviathan creates propaganda. Both the cells (individuals) of the superorganism and the society in which the superorganism lives must be reminded of the "good" mission of the superorganism, its *rationale*. Mission statements are always some variant of "Save the Children!" In the case of the VA, "Save the Veterans!" In the case of the NEA, "Save the Teachers and the Children!" In the case of GE, "Save the World!"

The propaganda organ of Leviathan asserts, "Leviathan is moral and good for humankind."

For many human actions there are rationales *and* reasons. The **rationale** is the story that is told to explain the thing. The **reason** is the true explanation for the thing. For example, the *reason* (the real truth of the matter) why the United States Federal Trade Commission and a multitude of other government agencies, foreign and domestic, want to regulate Uber, the ride-sharing service, is to cripple Uber for the benefit of the preexisting monopoly taxicab companies. The *rationale* (the lie told for public consumption to cover the avaricious motive) for the regulation is the safety of the passengers: "Save the Passengers!" The *freedom* of the passengers to choose[6] with whom they will do business is **not** the concern of Leviathan. In this respect—overriding the freedom of the individual customer to choose her service provider—Leviathan is immoral.

There are frequently a rationale (the lie) and a reason (the truth). The rationale for Leviathan is found in its mission statement. The reason for Leviathan is life and more life, regardless of mission, even in contravention of mission.

The propaganda organ of Leviathan communicates the rationale (the lie), not the reason (the truth), for Leviathan's existence. Leviathan's reason for being is life and more life for Leviathan without regard to morality, by any means.

Information Filter

"*His* scales *are his* pride, shut up together *as with* a close seal. One is so near to another, that no air can come between them" (Job 41:15–16).

Internal Information

Other organs of Leviathan filter information within the superorganism and into and out of the superorganism. The famous rule of spy organizations known as "need to know" is relevant in this context. Some internal information within Leviathan is shared on a "need to know" basis.

Consider, for example, an event occurring as this chapter is being composed. Volkswagen (VW), the German carmaker, is discovered to have allegedly introduced software into its cars that trick government emissions testing devices into concluding that the car being tested passes emissions standards. Obviously, this alleged activity is "off mission," assuming that VW's mission is something like "Make good cars for people." Illegal activity within a superorganism must be shared only on a "need to know" basis. Very powerful information filters, though ultimately unsuccessful in this case, must have been in place at VW for this alleged scheme to have been carried out, resulting in *millions* of VW vehicles being infected with illegal software.

The CEO of Peanut Corporation of America has recently been sentenced to twenty-eight years in federal prison for allegedly knowingly participating in the sale and distribution of salmonella-infected peanut butter product allegedly resulting in death and illness of customers. Surely, powerful information filters were at work in this company before these alleged crimes were exposed.

Not only must information filters be in place, but certain types of people must perform the tasks of the information filters. Leviathan needs criminals and sociopaths in certain highly sensitive functions. The information filters must conceal not only the criminal activity but also the employment of criminals and sociopaths to perform the criminal activities.

A sociopath is a person with a personality disorder characterized by anti-social behavior and a lack of conscience. Not all sociopaths are serial killers, like Ted Bundy. According to Dr. Martha Stout of Harvard University one in twenty-five Americans are sociopaths.[7] **Leviathan is always sociopathic**, lacking self-awareness and, therefore, *lacking a conscience.*

Keeping the antisocial, immoral, and sometimes illegal behavior of Leviathan secret from its nonsociopathic cells is crucial to the life and more life of Leviathan. In simple terms, most employees must believe that they are doing good by working for Leviathan.

Information Coming into or Going Out of the Superorganism

Information exists in the world. Leviathan has an organ that receives worldly input. Worldly inputs must be carefully filtered by Leviathan.

The National Ocean and Atmospheric Administration (NOAA), an agency of the United States Department of Commerce, monitors the environment, including world temperatures. NOAA's mission statement is "to understand and predict changes in climate, weather, oceans, and coasts, to share that knowledge and information with others, and to conserve and manage coastal and marine ecosystems and resources." Leviathan NOAA supports the currently wildly popular theory of manmade global warming.[8] Therefore, information from the environment that world temperatures have not risen in recent decades must be filtered. The information does not fit the organizational bias. Leviathan needs to massage the date, to send the data back to the field to be double checked, to leave it on the desk to be investigated later (years later or never), or simply to drop it in the trash can.[9] Like King Henry II (1133–1189) of England speaking about the Archbishop of Canterbury Thomas Becket (1118–1170), Leviathan says, "Who will rid me of this troublesome priest?" and Thomas Becket is assassinated. The offending data from the environment is gone. Or, when the data is uncooperative, Leviathan simply changes the name of the problem to "manmade *climate change*." Who doubts that the climate changes? Leviathan has its ways and means.

Large pharmaceutical companies are superorganisms. Data is constantly coming from the outside world. Studies are performed that might call into question the safety or effectiveness of drugs that are a source of billions of dollars of profits. If these studies are from sources that Leviathan directly controls, it might simply pocket the results, relying upon confidentiality agreements to keep study authors silent.[10] If the results cannot be suppressed, then the current result might be undermined by reference to other contradictory studies. Leviathan will never be concerned with harmful truths, only with a profitable outcome and a good reputation among its cells and in society. The presence of criminals and sociopaths within the external information filter organ comes in very handy.

The Centers for Disease Control and prevention (CDC) is a superorganism. The mission statement is to protect public health. Superorganisms work together for their own mutual continued existence. The cells of the CDC and of large pharmaceutical companies are often exchanged. A former director of the CDC allegedly resigned from the CDC (which recommends a broad spectrum of vaccinations). Later in the same year, she allegedly became the president of Merck's vaccine division.[11] The superorganism cell moved from Leviathan CDC to Leviathan Merck. Imagining that "regulated" Merck is independent of its "regulator" CDC is a popular fantasy.

In this context, the alleged statement of a CDC senior scientist in a press release[12] dated August 27, 2014, is not surprising:

> I regret that my coauthors and I omitted statistically significant information in our 2004 article published in the journal *Pediatrics*. The omitted data suggested that African American males who received the MMR vaccine before age 36 months were at increased risk for autism. Decisions were made regarding which findings to report after the data were collected, and I believe that the final study protocol was not followed.

Newswoman Sharyl Attkisson reports[13] that the CDC senior scientist allegedly testified to Congress:

> [We] scheduled a meeting to destroy documents related to the study. The remaining four co-authors all met and brought a big garbage can into the meeting room, and reviewed and went through all the hardcopy documents that we had thought we should discard, and put them into a huge garbage can.

"Who will rid me of this troublesome priest?" says Leviathan. The documents are destroyed by a senior scientist and his coconspirators.

Nor is it surprising that virtually no reader of this chapter will have heard this story. Why? The publishers of national news are also superorganisms. If one watches television, one sees that there are many paid advertisements for legal drugs for every conceivable medical and psychiatric condition. The mainstream media sell advertisements for legal drugs for a living. Leviathan ABC, NBC, CBS, CNN, MSNBC, FOX NEWS, and so on will not be paid by Leviathan Big Pharmaceutical or others unless alleged stories like this are suppressed or receive little or no play.

Unfortunately for Leviathan, Leviathan was allegedly exposed by its whistle-blowing[14] employee. But no matter, Leviathan has other ways to cover up uncooperative data, even once revealed. We never heard about it because Leviathan Mainstream Media does not widely, if at all, report the story. Furthermore, even having now heard about it, few people will believe it or be sufficiently intrigued to investigate further.

Not all large organizations are necessarily corrupt, just likely to be corrupt. All large organizations are superorganisms. All superorganisms are sociopathic, having no conscience. One in twenty-five people are sociopathic. An organization of 1,000 people is likely to have forty sociopathic employees. If the sociopaths are competent, they can find a place for themselves in the superorganism and their work will benefit the superorganism.

Remember the story of the Ring of Gyges in Plato's *Republic*. A shepherd finds the magical Ring of Gyges. If the ring is rotated down on the finger of the wearer, the wearer becomes invisible. The shepherd kills the king and marries the queen using the ring's power. (The magic ring trope appears again and again in literature; see *The Invisible Man* by H. G. Wells and *The Lord of the Rings* by J. R. R. Tolkien.) Plato's argument is that in the absence of the fear of discovery and punishment, people will commit horrible crimes for their advantage. The **competent sociopathic employee** is the equivalent of the shepherd possessing the Ring of Gyges. The competent sociopath can perform services for Leviathan, not necessarily killing the king and marrying the queen, but the business equivalents. Not being moral (being willing to steal for example) is an ***economic advantage*** if the thief is competent and therefore avoids detection and punishment. The reason normal people do not steal (besides the fear of discovery and punishment) is the fear of a bad conscience. The fear of a **bad conscience** is **more powerful** than the fear of discovery and punishment for nonsociopathic people. Posttraumatic stress syndrome among returning military service members is sometimes an extreme case of bad conscience. What can one do with one's life after killing a child in combat, even by accident?

Did well-placed sociopathic employees enable PCA, VW, and GSK to commit these alleged antisocial actions?

Human Resources (HR)

"When he raiseth up himself, the mighty are afraid: by reason of breakings they purify themselves. The sword of him that layeth at him cannot hold: the spear, the dart, nor the habergeon. He esteemeth iron as straw, *and* brass as rotten wood" (Job 41: 25–27).

Leviathan needs new cells (individuals), because old cells (individual employees) die. Therefore, Leviathan needs a human resources department. Leviathan must hire the right people in order to function.

Sometimes Leviathan needs criminals and sociopaths to form its cells. Only in the rarest case would a cell or organ within the superorganism intentionally hire a sociopath or a criminal. (The 1999 Mel Gibson film *Payback* has the crime boss explaining to his thug that the sociopathic thug was employed by the "Organization" precisely because the sociopath could torture and kill people without remorse.) As noted above, Dr. Martha Stout of Harvard University says that one in twenty-five Americans are sociopaths. Therefore, with any new hire there is a 4 percent chance of innocently employing a sociopath. Once employed, a competent sociopath becomes useful to Leviathan. Remember Leviathan is always a sociopath, lacking a conscience.

Leviathan is not self-conscious. Leviathan is like poison ivy. Leviathan just lives and grows in response to environmental inputs. No sun and water this way: death. Sun and water that way: life. The advancement of a sociopath through the superorganism will happen like plant growth or like successful organic mutations over generations in the case of evolution. (The successful random mutation results in a survival advantage to the organism with the mutation, resulting in a reproductive advantage for the mutated organism.) The adaption (employment of the sociopath) yields the required results (life and more life) for Leviathan. The sociopath moves to positions in the superorganism where his special talents are most needed. The sociopathic cell, **who is self-conscious**, but **without a conscience**, can participate in his strategic movement within the superorganism.

The employment of a competent sociopath who buys into the mission of Leviathan (life and more life, as opposed to living the *good* life) can be very useful to Leviathan. The sociopathic cell can do **whatever is necessary** to advantage Leviathan, and the sociopath's competence enables him to conceal his wrongdoing from other cells within the superorganism and from society at large. Normal people cannot tolerate feelings of guilt associated with immoral and illegal behavior and will avoid at all costs behaviors leading to a guilty conscience. Normal people will promptly confess their crimes in order to relieve their guilty consciences. Adam Smith (Scottish philosopher 1723–1790) famously said, "What can be added to the happiness of a man who is in health, out of debt, and has a clear conscience?" The longer Leviathan lives, the longer Leviathan has to accumulate useful sociopath cells.

The assassins of Thomas Becket who overheard King Henry II's plea, "Who will rid me of this troublesome priest?" were well placed sociopaths within the royal court.

Another factor in hiring is that normal people have a variety of moral standards. Libertarian—philosophically and morally opposed to the war on drugs—would never be able to function on moral grounds as a prosecutor whose job it is to imprison **insubordinate** people for decades for **victimless crimes**. Insubordinate (*malum prohibitum*) people are distinguished from people who steal from or physically injure (*malum in se*) others. Therefore, Libertarians are unlikely to seek employment with any government agency involved in the imprisonment of merely **insubordinate** people, such as the police, the prosecution, or the prison industry. A person opposed to abortion would never seek employment with Planned Parenthood Federation of America. A pacifist would never volunteer for the armed forces.

Different moral types are drawn to different superorganisms. Therefore, applicants present themselves to Leviathan having self-selected for Leviathan's mission.

Self-defense

"Lay thine hand upon him, remember the battle, do no more" (Job 41:8).

Superorganisms defend themselves. The existence of "whistle-blower" laws is a confession of the existence of this fact. A whistle-blower is a nonsociopathic employee (that is, a good person, an employee with a conscience) who has learned "need to know" information within his organization that is evidence of organizational "bad" behavior and who then reports that information to the public or to a regulatory agency.

Whistle-blowers are often isolated within organizations in order to ensure that they have no further contact with "need to know" information. Perhaps they are shipped to Timbuktu or the Alaskan outpost of the organization, anything to get them away from sensitive "need to know" information. Perhaps they are discredited. Leviathan hauls out every negative HR fact and makes it public.

Recently, a congressman's employment application to the United States Secret Service was allegedly used to embarrass the congressman, allegedly in retaliation for his participation in a congressional investigation of the United States Secret Service.[15] "Who will rid me of this troublesome congressman?"

An Internal Revenue Service employee retired following an investigation of alleged irregularities pertaining to the application by certain types of political entities for IRS 501(c)(4) tax-exempt status. "Who will rid me of these troublesome nonprofits?"

Presidential candidate Ben Carson was allegedly audited by the U.S. Internal Revenue Service (IRS) following his controversial television appearance with President Obama challenging America's leadership.[16] "Who will rid me of this troublesome doctor?"

On December 29, 1170, Thomas Becket, the Archbishop of Canterbury, was hacked to death by four knights of King Henry II of England, having heard the king utter the words "Who will rid me of this troublesome priest?" Who among us doubts that Leviathan will commit murder in self-defense even in these days?

We have identified five organs within Leviathan: propaganda, internal information filter, external information filter, human resources, and self-defense.

Let us now examine a particular set of superorganisms, governmental agencies.

Leviathan Big Government

"Upon earth there is not his like, who is made without fear. He beholdeth all high *things*: he *is* a king over all the children of pride" (Job 41:33–34).

Government is that organization having a monopoly over the use of force in a particular geographical area. The legitimate functions of government are the police, the courts, and national defense. Every other governmental activity is economic service to powerful constituencies. *Cui bono* (Latin: "who benefits") is the guiding light for all things governmental.

Governments, Aristotle teaches, can be of three general forms, rule by the one, rule by the few, or rule by the many. Each of these types can be good or bad. Therefore, there are six types of regimes according to Aristotle: monarchy, tyranny, aristocracy, oligarchy, polity, and democracy.

Aristotle's Politics

	Rule by the one	*Rule by the few*	*Rule by the many*
Good regime	Monarchy	Aristocracy	Polity
Bad regime	Tyranny	Oligarchy	Democracy

Good regimes are characterized by the good intentions of the ruler: **the good ruler is interested in the good of the community**. Bad regimes are characterized by the bad intentions of the ruler: **the bad ruler is interested in the good of the ruler**.

American government is an oligarchy. We are ruled by powerful, moneyed interests. *Cui bono*.

Almost every law or regulation currently enacted by city, state, and Federal Government legislatures or agencies benefits a powerful, moneyed constituency. Since there are thousands of laws and regulations enacted every year, the examples might go on forever. Here are a few.

On August 1, 2015, the PBS.org website had this headline: "Why is New York City cracking down on Airbnb?"[17] Why? New York hotels do not appreciate competition for tourist accommodation by homeowners in New York City. The upstart, Airbnb.com, is therefore suppressed in order to benefit the powerful, moneyed constituency, the hotel business.

On June 26, 2015, the BBC.org website[18] had this headline: "French Government orders Uber taxi ban after protests." Why? The taxicab industry in Paris does not appreciate competition for riders by private automobile owners. The upstart, Uber, is therefore suppressed in order to benefit the powerful, moneyed constituency.

On September 15, 2015, the Watchdog.org website[19] had this headline: "Pumping up Government: Washington, D.C. may regulate personal trainers." Why? Perhaps some powerful, moneyed constituency has whispered in the ear of some D.C. council member, "Who will rid me of these troublesome personal trainers?" Unless somebody's income was threatened by personal trainers, who would even think of such a thing?

The United States Transportation Security Administration (TSA) was created in response to the terrorist attacks in New York and Washington, D.C., on September 11, 2001. TSA's *rationale* (the lie) is "to protect the nation's transportation systems to ensure freedom of movement for people and commerce." The *reason* (the truth) is to protect airline profits. The government has taken over the security function from the airline business, and government imposes a direct tax on travelers for the service. On September 11, 2011, the CNN.com website[20] had this headline: "The 9/11 fund: Putting a price on life." The article stated that the 9/11 Fund [a fund created to compensate victims of 9/11] had a critical mandate: "To protect the airline industry from tanking and taking the U.S. economy down with it. Before the victims' families could receive funding, they had to agree to not sue the airlines." Here we have Leviathan Big Government protecting Leviathan Big Airlines. The reason (the truth): no superorganism can be allowed to fail (life and more life). The rationale: it's good for America to "Save the Children!" or to "Save the Airlines!"

Please note that **the "children" will be saved** in the absence of Leviathan. Leviathan Big Banks ("to big to fail"), Leviathan Big Pharmaceutical, Leviathan Big Agriculture, Leviathan Big Auto,

Leviathan Big Manufacturing, Leviathan Big Mining, Leviathan Big Defense, Leviathan Big Insurance, Leviathan Big Medical, and Leviathan Big Government **need not be saved.**

Whenever new laws are enacted, always check to see who benefits. **Cui bono**? Almost without exception, we will find that a powerful, moneyed constituency is benefiting from the new law. We may also find that the powerful, moneyed constituency has pushed for the new laws in nefarious ways. Fabian Libertarians must teach others to see these connections.

Leviathan Need Not Be Governmental

Leviathan usually is, but does not have to be, a government institution. Leviathan can be a nongovernment institution, but we will find that in order to be long-lived and large, a nongovernment institution will have **substantial governmental protection** in the form of subsidies, protective regulations, tax breaks, and monopoly rights. To call a government protected enterprise "private" is an Orwellian stretch of the English language.

Synonymous with the word "superorganism" when used to describe Leviathan is the phase "beyond human." **Leviathan is beyond human control.** Leviathan lives through its rules and regulations. A small private enterprise often has rules and regulations, but these rules and regulations are within the complete control of the entrepreneur. If an employee finds a glitch, he can approach his boss and tell her. The boss, being human and in control of her organization, can override or change the rules and regulations for that case or forever.

In large organizations, especially governmental organizations, no single employee has the power to change the rules and regulations. Even the internal organ responsible for making, monitoring, and changing the rules and regulations is strongly resisted in the case of any proposed change. Witness the allegedly unsuccessful efforts to change the internal operations of the Veterans Administration. Large bureaucracies are notoriously resistant to change.

A large corporation often has rules and regulations for its internal control. Large corporations often have barely accountable boards of directors supposedly responsible for making, monitoring, and changing the rules and regulations. Such a large corporation is a risk of becoming Leviathan. Many large corporations are Leviathan.

Conclusion

Our goal in this chapter was to explain how it is that so many societal problems are intractable. Now we know the reason: **Leviathan does not want the problems solved**. Thomas Edison's great invention, the incandescent light bulb, is outlawed in America because GE **can make more money** selling an expensive compact fluorescent light bulb (CFL) than it can by selling a cheap incandescent bulb. Veterans beloved of Americans are denied treatment by the VA unto death because the VA's mission is not to treat veterans but to provide lifetime employment and spectacular retirement benefits for government bureaucrats and to hand out lucrative contacts to favored providers (other superorganisms). Bad teachers are kept on indefinitely by a school system at full pay in isolated Temporary Reassignment Centers ("rubber rooms") in New York City because the teachers union's mission is not to provide a good education for children, but rather to provide lifetime employment and spectacular retirement benefits for government bureaucrats. *Cui bono*?

Heretofore we could not respond to superorganisms because of our lack of awareness of their existence. Now that we are aware, we continue to be hobbled by our relatively short life spans (compared with Leviathan), by our grossly inadequate Government Education, and by misinformation from Leviathan Mainstream Media which runs interference for all superorganisms.

We have taken a first responsive step to superorganisms in this chapter by revealing the existence of Leviathan. Our next step must be to become like the ancient yeoman farmer and act with decades and centuries in mind, being prepared to pass our legacy on to our decedents. In this context, our legacy is our new awareness of Leviathan and our soon-to-be-developed strategies to destroy it. We must refresh our knowledge history and philosophy. The founding fathers of America received the right lessons in the form of a Classical Education. We too can seek a Classical Education and provide it to our children. Finally, we must learn to listen to Leviathan Mainstream Media, understanding that we are hearing and seeing, whatever it is that we are hearing and seeing, because *someone wants us* to hear and see it in order that **that someone** can benefit from our hearing and seeing. We need to ask, "*cui bono?*" of all that we see and hear.

In the next chapter, we will learn about a special superorganism, Leviathan Education.

Chapter 2—Leviathan Education

The Key to Utopia: Government Education

Government Education of the young has always been the key to Utopia. From the first public reading of Plato's *Republic* in fourth century BC in ancient Athens until today, the favored theoretical method for engineering the hoped-for society has been **government controlled** education of the young. The modern American view of Government Education is captured in the following quotation from the Father of Democratic Totalitarianism, Jean-Jacques Rousseau (1712–1778).

> L'éducation publique, sous des règles prescrites par le Gouvernement, et sous des magistrats établis par le Souverain est donc une des maximes fondamentales du Gouvernement populaire ou légitime. Si les enfants sont élevés en commun dans le sein de l'égalité, s'ils sont imbus des lois de l'Etat et des maximes de la volonté générale, s'ils sont instruits à les respecter par-dessus toutes choses, s'ils sont environnés d'exemples et d'objets qui leur parlent sans cesse de la tendre mère qui les nourrit, de l'amour qu'elle a pour eux, des biens inestimables qu'ils reçoivent d'elle, et du retour qu'ils lui doivent, ne doutons pas qu'ils n'apprennent ainsi à se chérir mutuellement comme des frères, à ne vouloir jamais que ce que veut la société, à substituer des actions d'hommes et de citoyens au stérile et vain babil des sophistes, et à devenir un jour les défenseurs et les pères de la patrie dont ils auront été si long-tems les enfants. [Discours sur l'Economie Politique by Jean-Jacques Rousseau, 1758]

> Public education, under rules prescribed by the Government and by the magistrates established by the sovereign, is therefore one of the fundamental maxims of popular and legitimate Government. If the children are raised in common in the heart of equality, if **they are imbued with the laws of the state and the maxims of the general will**, if they are instructed to respect those things above all else, if they are surrounded by examples and objects that speak to them ceaselessly of the tender mother that nourishes them, of the love that she has for them, of the inestimable goods that they receive from her and, on their part, that they therefore owe her, we do not doubt that they will thus learn to cherish one another as brothers, to want only that which society wants, to substitute the actions of men and citizens for the sterile and vain babble of the sophists, and to become one day the defenders and the fathers of the country of which they will have been for such a long time the children. (Emphasis supplied. Author's translation.)

Rousseau wants to create children who want only what "society" wants. Substitute "Leviathan" for "society" and we have the theme of this chapter. Leviathan wants children who want what Leviathan wants. Leviathan wants life and more life for Leviathan, not the ***good*** life (a moral and happy life).

Sociopathic Leviathan

We will recall from the previous chapter that Leviathan is not self-conscious and therefore has no conscience. Leviathan does not plan evil. Leviathan does not "plan" at all. Rather those actions that promote life and more life for Leviathan are "selected" over the very long life of Leviathan. Advantageous actions are selected ***without regard*** to their moral worth or lack thereof. Leviathan is, by definition, a sociopath[21], meaning lacking a conscience.

Remember that, according to Dr. Martha Stout of Harvard University, one in twenty-five people is a sociopath. Government Education is the largest superorganism on the planet. According to the National Center for Education Statistics[22], there were 3.5 million full-time teachers in elementary and secondary schools in 2013. According to the Department for Professional Employees of the AFL-CIO[23], there were 804,000 education administrators in 2013. Who knows how many janitors, cafeteria workers, security officers, counselors, and so on, there are? Our count of educators excludes teachers, educator, administrators, and staff of college, graduate, and postgraduate schools. Simply for the sake of argument, if there are 5 million people in the education business, and if one in twenty-five of all people is a sociopath, we are likely to have two hundred thousand sociopaths in the education business, helping Leviathan Education to achieve life and more life for Leviathan.

That, of course, leaves 4.8 million people who are not sociopaths in the education business. Most of the author's family, including the author, are in the education business. We have unbounded respect for teachers. For many teachers, teaching is a true calling. They are good at teaching and they love the work. Many teachers love teaching so much that they do it for free. **The good and moral teacher is the rule**, rather than the exception.

That said, recall that sociopaths rise within large superorganisms because competent sociopaths can most effectively promote the life and more life of Leviathan. Remember the reason: sociopaths can do **anything** to succeed: lie, cheat, steal, act unjustly, and even commit murder. Sociopathic individuals are not constrained by conscience, lacking the same. Leviathan is by definition sociopathic. Highly competent sociopaths might rise very high in the management of Leviathan. The **longer** the superorganism has lived, the more likely it is that sociopaths are in positions of authority. The **larger** the superorganism is, the more likely it is that sociopaths are in positions of authority.

Leviathan's Mission

Leviathan always has a rationale for its existence (the lie) and a reason for its existence (the truth). The reason for Leviathan's existence is life and more life. Life and more life mean power and money. The rationale for its existence varies. In the case of Leviathan

Education, the rationale for its existence is to educate the children. ***"Save the children!"***

The education of children is undoubtedly a sacred task. Children are sacred. Ask any parent. Educating children to adulthood is **the task** of parenting.

Leviathan's organ of propaganda teaches that the sacred mission of Leviathan Education is to teach the children. The sacred nature of the parental responsibility to teach their children is co-opted by Leviathan Education. Therefore, many people believe that Leviathan Education is a sacred institution. Because of the virtual worship of Government Education, the improvement of education will happen with glacial slowness and will not come to fruition until toward the end of the one-hundred-years plan herein set forth.

That Leviathan Education fails in its alleged mission to teach the children is clear from the graduation rates in many large public school systems. In Clayton County, Georgia, for example, the high school graduation rate was 55.8 percent in 2013–2014. Any alleged graduation rate is engineered and filtered by the information filters of Leviathan Education. What an actual high school "graduate" is capable of doing is by no means clear from the graduation rate. Hopefully, the "graduate" can at least read on a sixth-grade level.

All Leviathan need do vis-à-vis its mission is to give the appearance of performing the same. In the case of Leviathan Education, Leviathan presents **Education Theater**. In the case of airport security (TSA), Leviathan TSA presents **Airport Security Theater**. In the case of the CDC, Leviathan CDC presents **Healthcare Theater**.

The cost of education varies across the United States from over $30,000 per student per year in the Newark Public Schools to $6,260 per student per year in Idaho Falls School District 91.

According to ballotpedia.org[24], the highest expenditures per student in 2014 were made by the Newark Public Schools, New Jersey, (NPS)[25] at $30,742 per student. Newark Public Schools employ 5,595 people, have 66 schools, and have 35,054 students. Eight unions represent various subsets of employees. NPS's origin dates back to AD 1676. The 2014 graduation rate in 2014 was 68.8 percent, with no breakout of those who "graduated" through "nontraditional" pathways. In 2013, the nontraditional rate was 26 percent, and the

High School Proficiency Assessment (HSPA) rate was 42 percent, the sum being 68 percent, quite close to the 2014 total rate.

The lowest expenditures per student in 2014 were made by the Idaho Falls School District 91, Idaho[26], at $6,260 per student. This school district has 18 schools and 10,200 students. More than 90 percent of the students graduate from high school.

At $30,000 per year, every Newark child's parents might employ the great philosopher Aristotle (384–322 BC) as a full-time tutor for their child as did the parents of Alexander the Great (356–323 BC). No one can doubt that **something other** than educating the children is going on in Newark.

Both of the author's children attend nongovernment schools. Each school costs the parents about $10,000 per year, though one of the tuitions is supplemented by another $10,000 in scholarships. Both schools teach children from age two and one-half through high school graduation. The staff at one school for the entire student body numbering about seventy-six children is ten (a Montessori school). The staff at the other for the entire student body numbering seventy-six children is forty-seven (a special-needs school).

Why Is Leviathan Wicked?

Because the stated missions of all Leviathans are good (they are designed to be), we need to understand why Leviathan is wicked. We are analyzing Leviathan Education.

Leviathan Education is wicked because it denies parents the sacred right to educate their children.

Leviathan Education has customers—the parents of the children who attend public schools. These customers generally are required to use the services of Leviathan Education. First, there are mandatory school attendance laws. Parents **must** send their children to school. Second, parents are **taxed** by the government to support Leviathan Education. The imposition of the education tax reduces the funds available to parents to choose nongovernment educational options. Many parents cannot afford to pay education taxes and also pay tuition at nongovernment schools. Most parents could not afford to pay for nongovernment school tuition even in the absence of the education tax. (Just imagine the range of opportunities for the children of Newark if *even one-half* of the $30,000 per student per year spent by the government on Leviathan Education were made available to the parents to buy educational services at institutions *of their own choosing*.)

Leviathan Education has a practical monopoly on the education of children. In 2013, about 90 percent of American children attended public schools.[27] Since Leviathan Education has a government imposed monopoly, Leviathan Education need only be superficially concerned with the rationale (the lie) for its existence.

At a nongovernment school, when the customers are not satisfied, they can move their children to another school or home school. When parents are dissatisfied with their government school and they cannot afford the nongovernment alternative, their only option may be to move to better government school districts. Of course, many people do choose to live in the best government school districts. Some people lie about their addresses (a crime) to get their children into the best government schools. Some parents grant temporary guardianship over their children to a relative who lives in a good school district.

All of these limitations on normal customer relations mean that Leviathan Education need be only superficially concerned with its stated mission: to educate the children. Education Theater is entirely sufficient for this purpose.

Given that Leviathan Education is not really mission driven (to educate the children), what does it do instead? Leviathan Education is concerned with life and more life. Life and more life mean money and power. Leviathan Education seeks to increase its size and budget. Naturally, Leviathan Education opposes nongovernment schools furiously. There is no greater threat to Leviathan Education than nongovernment alternatives to education.

The resources that Leviathan Education can bring to the war against nongovernment education are practically unlimited. Besides the full support of Leviathan Education's internal organs—propaganda, information filters, HR, and self-defense—Leviathan Education will be joined in its war against nongovernment education by every other Leviathan with or without invitation. ***The greatest threat to Leviathans is a threat to their monopoly power.***

Leviathan Education will go to any lengths to keep the pretense of education, Education Theater, going. In 2015, eleven government school teachers in Georgia were convicted of racketeering for allegedly falsifying student test results.[28] This scandal is entirely ***unsurprising*** given the nature of Leviathan and its organs.

Who Works for Leviathan?

There are a number of types of individuals who work for Leviathan: Innocents, Time Markers, Stars, Innovators, Slugs, and Sociopaths.

Innocents

Most employees of Leviathan Education fall into this category: Innocents. The existence of Leviathan was not heretofore known. Therefore, few people are aware of the sociopathic superorganisms that run, undermine, and ruin our lives. Very few people are aware of Dr. Martha Stout's claim that one in twenty-five people is a sociopath. Most people are good. Most people are innocent. One wonders for how long Innocents remain innocent. After years working for Leviathan Education, Innocents cannot avoid meeting the other types. Innocents ultimately become Time Markers.

Time markers

After a short stint as an Innocent, employees of Leviathan become Time Markers.

Commonly, government jobs are well paid in relation to nongovernment employment. Government employees are often protected by Leviathan Union. Government employees are often protected by civil service regulations. Government employees often hold their jobs as a matter of right and cannot easily be fired. We mentioned the Temporary Reassignment Centers ("rubber rooms")[29] in New York City in chapter 1. Government employees often enjoy a host of Leviathan-provided employee benefits, like health insurance and retirement plans. These benefits have the effect of tying Leviathan employees to their jobs. In the current work environment, a good government job is the equivalent of winning the lottery: lifetime security.

Government employees will therefore endure much to keep their jobs. Employees of Leviathan are not likely to become whistleblowers. They will not call attention to Slug employees. They will not disclose the practice of "buying paper clips." They will not disclose the employment of useless and unneeded employees. They will not usually disclose or oppose minor (or even major) abuse of fellow employees by Leviathan. They might not even disclose violations of the law.

In any event, to whom would any such disclosure be made? Almost always to Leviathan. The story of the slandered, libeled, shunned, ostracized, persecuted, sued, and prosecuted whistle-blower is well known. Consider the fate of the infamous whistle-blower Edward Snowden. Consider the poisoning of Alexander Litvinenko[30] by lethal polonium-210.

Many good people working for Leviathan do their jobs quietly. They keep their heads down and their eyes and ears averted. They mind their own business. They do not volunteer. They turn their attention away from questionable activities, whether illegal or immoral. "See no evil, hear no evil, speak no evil." They do their time until retirement and slink away thankful for having avoided punishment, or excessive guilt for having turned a blind eye.

They keep telling themselves that the mission of Leviathan is good. They ignore the wicked reality of their master.

Stars

Star employees are highly valued in nongovernment employment in which the customer relations is crucial. To Leviathan, the customer is a nuisance. Pleasing the customer is the only way for a private enterprise to survive. Leviathan has a government monopoly and need not concern itself, other than superficially, with the customer.

The Star employee is always ready to advance the mission of the organization. For example, in the case of a small family sandwich shop in a strip mall, the mission is to create delicious sandwiches quickly for customers in a clean and friendly environment. The Star employee is always smiling. She is eager to help the customers. She knows many customers by name. She is meticulous in the execution of her tasks. In the absence of an immediate task, she looks for tasks to perform. In a slow moment at the customer counter, she visits the restrooms to make sure they are clean and stocked. Her absence from work is immediately noticed by the regular customers. If she quit, some regulars might start looking for another place to eat lunch.

Every entrepreneur longs for Star employees. Every entrepreneur is anxious to keep the Star employee happy at work.

On the other hand, Leviathan despises the Star employee. The Star employee reveals the inadequacy of Leviathan simply by being there. Star employees are rare. The presence of one Star accents the absence of good customer relations in other parts of Leviathan.

Other employees of Leviathan envy and resent the Star employee. The Star employee's supervisor will actively seek to rein in the Star. The supervisor might even explicitly say to the Star, "Tone it down a little. Showing up the others hurts employee morale." The coemployees of the Star employee will take every opportunity to undermine the Star. They will talk behind her back. They will spread false rumors about her. They will close her out-of-office parties and off-site events. The Star employee is likely to be shunned by other employees of Leviathan. For these reasons, the Star employee is unhappy and short-lived within Leviathan.

Leviathan has no need of Star employees who serve the customers with excellence.

Innovators

Anyone who has ever attempted to make changes in a bureaucracy will be painfully aware the Innovators are not welcome in Leviathan. Suggestion boxes are present in some bureaucracies, but the adoption of employee suggestions is rare. Within Leviathan the suggestion box is merely **_Good Management Theater_**.

Remember Leviathan has a rationale for being (the lie) and reason for being (the truth). The rationale for Leviathan Education is to teach children (the lie). The reason for being is life and more life (the truth). Honest Innovators will be thinking about the rationale for being and therefore their suggestions will be directed toward how to improve teaching the children. Such suggestions are unwelcomed.

Of course, a suggestion as to how to improve **Education Theater** would always be welcome by Leviathan Education. One wonders which (dishonest) "innovator" in the Atlanta Public School system first allegedly suggested to the alleged coconspirators that they surreptitiously alter student test results to improve the scores by cheating.

Entrepreneurs love Innovators and the consequent opportunity to improve customer relations. In the private sector, great Innovators might implement their own ideas by becoming entrepreneurs themselves. Innovators within Leviathan Education are less likely to strike out on their own because of the monopoly held by Leviathan Education.

To give credit where credit is due, recall the 1988 film *Stand and Deliver* staring Edward James Olmos. The film fictionalizes the excellent work of government schoolteacher Jaime Escalante. Mr. Escalante was a greater teacher who, in a Los Angeles County government school, spearheaded a calculus program resulting in minority students taking AP Calculus courses and passing the AP Calculus exam, contrary to the expectations of many.

In general, Innovators are not welcome in Leviathan. Jaime Escalante was not welcomed by all of his colleagues. Jaime Escalante is the exception to the rule.

Slugs

Slug employees are not a problem in Leviathan. Leviathan cares about its budget in the sense that Leviathan wants a large budget, in contrast to private enterprise that always seeks to cut costs. A Slug employee is a perfect addition to the staff of Leviathan. The Slug's performance is not resented by anyone for its excellence. The Slug does not innovate. The Slug does not volunteer. The Slug does not help his coemployees. The Slug interacts with customers as little as possible. Furthermore, the absence of work product from the Slug is good for Leviathan because **work not done** provides justification for more employees and, therefore, a larger payroll.

Employers within Leviathan will even hire more Slugs *as slugs*. Most employees and former employees of government bureaucracies will recognize the phenomenon of "buying paper clips." Some managers of government bureaucracies will, at the end of the budget year, make sure to spend the remaining supply budget even if supplies are not needed in order that upper management will not cut the underling's budget. "Buying paper clips" may even be an organization-wide policy, if the budget is decided by a government agency outside Leviathan (like the state Legislature). Life and more life mean power and money. Leviathan's expenditure of money must never decrease, only increase. Of course, in a private enterprise the exact opposite philosophy applies. Cost-cutting measures are always sought by private enterprise in order to increase profits.

A variation of "buying paper clips" applies to Leviathan's employment practices. Sometimes interns, part-time or even full-time, are employed for no apparent reason. On the government budget theory of use-it-or-lose-it, some government managers will hire unneeded employees. With nothing productive to do, the employees might be tasked with reading books and writing book reports (at least superficially related to Leviathan's mission statement, one hopes). Leviathan has been known to hire people for the express purpose of being a Slug. Remember the $30,000 per student per year budget of the Newark Public Schools.

Most Slugs are not specially hired for the job of being a Slug. Most Slugs are just Slugs. Slugs commonly surf the Internet and do online shopping at work when not pretending to work.

Sociopaths

One in twenty-five people is a sociopath. A sociopath is a person who has no conscience. The competent sociopath can, within the scope his competence, do anything, moral or not, to accomplish his goals. Good social behavior is controlled by fear of punishment and by fear of a bad conscience. Bad conscience is by far the most powerful control of social behavior in the case of nonsociopaths. The opportunities to commit little crimes without fear of punishment are manifold in life. Most people do not take those opportunities because of the fear of bad conscience. ***A good person values a clear conscience above all else!*** "What can be added to the happiness of a man who is in health, out of debt, and has *a clear conscience*?" Adam Smith (1723–1790).

It is difficult to understate the danger we are in with one of twenty-five people around us likely to be a sociopath.

Within a large organization, the sociopaths can do great harm to other employees. The Stars and the Innovators are at greatest risk. Anyone to whom attention is drawn is a possible target for a sadistic sociopath. If the sociopath is a person's manager, woe unto the unfortunate employee.

Sociopaths are useful in the information filter organ of Leviathan. The filtering of relevant information into and out of the organization can come very close to lying. A person without a conscience can be a great liar. Remember the 2015 VW scandal involving the alleged programming of VW automobiles to cheat emissions testing. Many lies must have been told to keep that secret.

Sociopaths are useful in the self-defense organ of Leviathan. Russian Alexander Litvinenko was poisoned. Thomas Becket (1119–1170) was hacked to death by the knights of King Henry II of England (1133–1189). In modern politics, while murder is still an option, political and character assassinations are the preferred method of enforcement. Remember the attempts to destroy United States Supreme Court Justice Clarence Thomas during his 1991 U.S. Senate confirmation hearings and the destruction of the presidential candidacy of Herman Cain in 2012.

Conclusion

This chapter began with a quotation from Jean-Jacques Rousseau. Rousseau refers to the General Will (*la volonté générale*). The idea of the General Will is as close to God as Rousseau comes. American society has thoroughly absorbed Rousseau's idea. In fact, in our increasingly secular society, the idea of the General Will has overtaken the idea of God. The idea of the General Will underlies America's belief that the right to vote is Freedom itself.

Because America has voted itself Leviathan Education, Americans believe that Leviathan Education is sanctioned by the General Will. Tie this "sacred" mandate by the General Will with the asserted sacred mission of Leviathan Education—to educate the children—and we have a superorganism that is presently invulnerable.

Most teachers are good people. Some teachers are great. Not all government schools are equally bad. The closer the government administrators and teachers are to the parents, the better the school is likely to be. Parents are closer to their government schools in small jurisdictions. Middle-class parents are closer to their government schools in general. Therefore, some readers may not recognize the monsters described in this chapter. Be assured, though, Leviathan Education exists.

Leviathan Education is evil because it essentially forbids most parents the right to educate their children. All parents are required by law to educate their children. Most parents cannot afford nongovernment alternatives. The goal of Leviathan Education is not to educate children, but rather to give life and more life to Leviathan. No expense is spared.

Chapter 3—Economics

We need a basic understanding of economics in order to execute our one-hundred-years plan to restore American Freedom. What follows is simple to understand.

The Simple Rules of Economics

The word "economics" comes from the Greek, *Τα Οἰκονομικά* (Latinized form, *Oeconomica*), the title of a treatise attributed to Aristotle (384–322 BC). Aristotle's title means "household management."

Rule 1

Leviathan benefits when economics is a mystery. Scottish philosopher Thomas Carlyle (1795–1881) called economics the "dismal science." The complex mathematics and statistics associated with economics contribute to the murkiness of the subject. Economics though can be simple. According Aristotle, a fundamental principle of household management is that household **expenditures must be kept within the limits of income** (*Economics*, 1346a[31]). The rules that apply to household economics apply equally to government economics. Leviathan's failure to follow this principle is alone sufficient to discredit Leviathan.

Rule 2

Another simple rule of economics is the **supply-demand-price relationship**. The model states that a free-market price varies in relation to supply and demand and that the price will stabilize at a point at which supply and demand are equal.

Demand-Price Example

Here is a demand-price example. Imagine that a city's power grid is destroyed by a hurricane. People in need of power in the hurricane-damaged city quickly buy all the electric power generators in the area. The price of electric power generators quadruples, from $1,000 to $4,000. Entrepreneurs from cities 500 or 1,000 miles away buy electric power generators readily available in their cities for $1,000 and deliver them to the hurricane-damaged city to sell for $4,000. This is, of course, illegal in most states. Anti-price-gouging laws are economically irrational, but make perfect sense to Leviathan. ***Demand goes up. Price goes up***. Supply rises in response to the price going up.

If the government is successful in enforcing its anti-price-gouging laws, there will be no generators for the hurricane-damaged city except those donated.

Supply-Price Example

Here is a supply-price example. Imagine that a new technology for extracting oil from the ground is discovered, say hydraulic fracturing, or "fracking." Fracking involves the injection of water, sand, and chemicals into an oil well to cause the gas to flow more freely to the wellhead. ***Supply goes up. Price goes down***. As of this writing (2016), gasoline is approaching one dollar per gallon in some states (gasoline is under one dollar per gallon in Michigan), after reaching almost $8 per gallon in July 2008.

With these simple rules of economics in mind, this chapter explores a number of current economic subjects: minimum wage, household servants, healthcare, depression, and costs associated with supply.

Minimum Wage

The author formed a short-lived discussion group called "Does Reason Work?" The group decided to tackle the subject of the "Minimum Wage: Good Policy or Bad?" Of all the popular economic debates, the subject of the minimum wage seems easily resolvable by application of the supply-demand-price rule. After two meetings, the group dissolved concluding that reason did not work. People are not persuadable on this issue.

Libertarians, of course, believe in freedom generally, and in free enterprise specifically. This section is therefore directed toward non-Libertarians with the goal of persuading them that ***freedom of employment*** is a good thing.

The minimum wage amounts to a command from government that certain people may not work even though employers exist who would employ them. Understand this precisely: ***the minimum wage forbids employment to certain types of people***.

Most good people who support the minimum wage do so because they think the minimum wage helps poor people (a subset of the "Little People" discussed in another chapter). Most good, educated people who support the minimum wage are not shills of Leviathan. They are not sociopaths supporting their Leviathan in order to advance themselves within their sociopathic superorganism knowing full well the harm the minimum wage does. They are simply good people who do not understand the simple rules of economics stated here and who have been taken in by the sociopathic shills of Leviathan. They are the victims of decades of miseducation or noneducation by Leviathan.

Wages Are Prices

Wages are, simply, one of many prices. Wages are the price employers pay for the performance of certain tasks. The completion of the tasks has a specific value to the employer. If a job is worth three dollars per hour for its performance and not four dollars per hour, then an employer will only hire the job out for three dollars per hour or less. If the government forbids a willing employee and a willing employer to contract for three dollars per hour, then the employee will remain unemployed and the employer will find a substitute nonhuman asset to perform the task, will perform the task himself, or will forego the doing of the task entirely.

There are many economic variables, but let us think of a few examples.

Retired Lady Example

A retired person would enjoy the opportunity to be productive in her golden years. She has no need of income because she saved for retirement and is living comfortably on her savings. She simply wants to be useful. A young family needs a babysitter for their newborn so that both parents can continue to work. The family can only afford two dollars per hour. The retired lady and the young family are forbidden to contract on these terms in every state in the Union. The government **forbids** this **voluntary relationship** between retired lady and young family.

Unpaid College Intern

A young college student, still in school, fully supported by her parents, would like experience working in the entertainment industry in New York City. An unpaid internship would be perfect for the student. She can get to know the people in the industry. She can experience the type of work required. She can discover whether her life's calling is, indeed, in the entertainment industry. The enterprise would benefit by training a potential employee and by screening a potential future employee at a relatively low cost. (Even though there is no wage for this hypothetical intern, there are always costs associated with interns, like training, office space, office supplies, liability insurance, the risk of lawsuits for violations of federal and state employment laws, and the like.) The enterprise might also get some real work done, though internships are more often about good works, good will, and relationship building, rather than about productivity or profit for the enterprise. Unless the enterprise granting the internship complies with United States Department of Labor "informal guidelines" consisting of six factors as interpreted by the federal courts,[32] the unpaid internship cannot exist. The government *forbids* this ***voluntary relationship*** between student and enterprise. The very existence of these "informal guidelines" and the necessity to consult an attorney about compliance is an enormous deterrent to creating unpaid internships, and this result, limiting the ***supply*** of labor, benefits Leviathan and its constituencies.

Unemployed Young Adult

A young adult (over eighteen), still living at home, would like to get off the couch in his mother's basement, and get into the workforce to start his life as an independent, self-sufficient adult. Since he lives with his mommy, he needs no income. He has graduated from high school, can read, and can perform simple arithmetic. He has common sense. He has had a good upbringing by his parents, and he is therefore honest, clean, physically fit, and able to meet his commitments (he can get to work on time). His family lives in a jurisdiction with a high minimum wage, more than double the federal minimum wage. The young adult would benefit by spending forty hours per week ***off the couch***, away from the basement television set and his video games in a clean, temperature-controlled, brightly lighted, safe, bustling, and friendly workplace. He would learn important skills and begin to establish a reputation as a valuable employee. He would learn how to interact with a variety of people, customers, suppliers, coemployees, and supervisors. He might find his true calling. He would learn about the workaday world and civil society. He would be on the road to independent adult citizenship. Because the work he can do for the available employers is worth less than the minimum wage, he remains in his mother's basement in front of the television set. The government *forbids* this ***voluntary relationship*** between young unemployed man and retailer.

Leviathan's Strawman

The strawman, supplied by Leviathan's shills, of the pro-minimum-wage argument looks something like this: Two young parents, good people, with two young children, work fifty to sixty hours per week each at multiple minimum wage jobs to make ends meet. They have healthcare insurance through work (thanks to Obamacare). They are lucky to have retired parents who are able to help some with childcare, though they still have to pay for forty hours of childcare each week for their two children. The children go to public school. At the federal minimum wage of $7.25 per hour, the parents gross $800 per week together. After various government withholdings, they take home $600 per week together. They make $2,600 per month or $31,200 per year, or about 123 percent of the 2015 Federal Poverty Guidelines. Daycare costs them $1,944 per month, leaving them with $756 per month to live on. That amount must cover everything else including food, clothing, shelter, utilities, transportation, deductibles and co-pays for healthcare, and so on. This scenario is impossible. The little family cannot live on $756, which is less than their rent and utilities. Doubling their wages by doubling the federal minimum wage increases their take home pay to $3,356, which is doable.

The strawman scenario overlooks many issues. The biggest issue is whether the couple's four minimum wage employers can afford to double the couple's wages. Even if the employers could (as an act of charity), would they choose to do so (to be charitable)? Another issue avoided is that this hypothetical couple violated the oldest written rule of household management: **Household expenditures must be kept within the limits of income**. Rule 1. The scenario fails to explain why responsible parents would undertake the sacred task of parenting without the financial means to do so? The scenario omits any discussion of Freedom. By what right does Leviathan Big Government mandate that two parties, employer and employee, can enter into a *voluntary* employment contract **only on terms set by Leviathan**?

Consequences of the Minimum Wage

What does the minimum wage look like in practice?

1. **Unemployment**, especially in case of young minorities. In 2015, the unemployment rate for African American youth was 51 percent.[33]
2. Many people on government assistance.

3. Coin laundries.
4. Automatic teller machines (ATM).
5. Electronic payment kiosks at airport parking and elsewhere.
6. Supermarket self-checkout stations.
7. Pay-at-the-pump gas stations.
8. Automobile rental without humans, à la Zipcar.com.
9. Computer tablets on restaurant tables *in lieu of* waiters and waitresses.
10. Automatic snack dispensers in movie theaters and elsewhere.
11. Automatic propane gas tank dispensing machines at big box home improvement stores.
12. Automatic boarding-pass kiosks in airports and train stations.
13. Automated telephone trees and voice mail for customer service.
14. Brick-and-mortar retail stores, including their salespeople, replaced by Amazon.com and other online retailers.
15. Brick-and-mortar vocational schools, junior colleges, colleges, and universities replaced by online educational services.
16. Computer-generated music replacing musicians and orchestras, even in live New York Theater and at the ballet.
17. Digital music and videos replacing CDs and DVDs.
18. Online streaming replacing movie theaters and other entertainment venues.
19. Security camera surveillance in lieu of human security guards.
20. Intersection cameras automatically issuing stoplight violation tickets replacing policemen.
21. Robotic factories.
22. Machines that milk cows.
23. Machines that till the soil.
24. Machines that plant crops.
25. Machines that harvest crops.
26. Manufacturing jobs moved overseas to China, Mexico, or elsewhere.
27. White-collar jobs outsourced via the Internet to India or elsewhere.
28. Self-directed legal services provided online by computers.
29. Self-directed medical laboratory services provided online.

30. Digitized actors replacing human actors (not yet a reality).
31. Self-driving cars (not yet a reality).

Libertarians Are Not Luddites

Libertarians are not Luddites, and the foregoing list of improvements in productivity should not be misinterpreted as suggesting that Libertarians oppose progress. **Progress is good**. Progress, though, changes the supply-demand-price relationships, and people must be free to respond to changes in these factors in order to make sound economic judgments. All of the listed improvements are entrepreneurial responses to high prices, including wages, and the improvements result in lower prices. ***The general trend in a free-market economy of all prices, including wages, is down!***[34]

Sound economic judgments are made in response to a rising free-market price by finding a lower-priced alternative or substitute product, doing without the product, or manufacturing the product oneself. Of course, there are many options available to customers and entrepreneurs in a free market.

The Total Cost of Labor

A concluding observation on the subject of minimum wage is necessary. Thus far we have spoken of the hourly wage *rate* only. However, the employer is concerned with the total cost of employment, not merely the wage *rate*. In addition to a minimum hourly wage, there are many other factors—taxes, employee benefits, and regulations—that increase the total cost of employment. For example,

1. worker's compensation insurance;
2. state and federal unemployment taxes;
3. Social Security taxes (both employer and employee contribution);
4. local, state, and federal income taxes;
5. healthcare insurance;
6. life insurance;

7. disability insurance;
8. pension plans;
9. 401(k) plans;
10. regulatory requirements required preemployment such as federally mandated citizenship check (IRS Form I-9) or drug testing;
11. regulatory requirements required during employment, such has government mandated vacations, sick leaves, family leaves, work condition regulations, hours of employment, number of hours worked, overtime, and so on;
12. regulatory requirements required to terminate employment; and
13. expenses and regulations imposed by Leviathan Union.

All of these taxes, employee benefits, and regulations increase the total cost of employment, as do increases in the minimum wage. Some of these extras are necessary only in the case of full-time employment, thus the current popularity among employers for part-timers.

Conclusion on the Minimum Wage

The first consequence of the minimum wage is unemployment, the ***denial by law of employment to willing employees***. The second consequence of the minimum wage is to incentivize employers to lower costs by finding nonhuman solutions to the tasks that human employees used to perform.

The result hoped for the True Believer in the minimum wage will never be, ***cannot be as a matter of economic law***, the long-term employment of a person at a price greater than the value of the employee's work. This principle is so simple. It is stupefying that Leviathan's subjects fail to understand. Maybe reason really does not work.

Household Servants

Middle-class Americans do not have servants. In many Third World countries middle-class families do have servants. In America, even the word "servant" is pejorative. Servant means household maid, personal maid, butler, valet, nanny, gardener or groundskeeper, and chauffeur. There is nothing wrong with being someone's household servant. In fact, until some entrepreneur invents androids, personal service jobs may be the last frontier of human employment. The butler, the chauffeur, the gardener, the maid, and the nanny cannot be outsourced to India.

Some readers may recall "Nannygate." In 1993, nominees to federal posts were denied Senate confirmation when it was discovered that they had hired illegal aliens—in one case a nanny and a chauffeur— and failed to pay Social Security taxes. Apart from violating the Social Security law, there is nothing wrong with employing a nanny and a chauffeur. Certainly, part of the denied nominees' problem was the apparent hypocrisy of seeking a federal office while violating federal law. In a Libertarian world, there would be no "illegal" aliens and there would be no Social Security tax.

Thousands of new household service jobs would open up in the absence of the minimum wage and the layers of taxes and regulations upon employment.

The supply-demand-price relationship implies that in a free-market economy, all people who wanted to work (the *supply*) would be employed (the *demand*) at some price (the *price*). In a free-market economy, the unemployment rate would be zero. (Because in a free-market economy people can easily move from employment to employment, there would be some temporary unemployment during moves.)

Healthcare

We mentioned healthcare above as one of the benefits to which full-time employees are entitled as a matter of federal and state law. In this section, we will discuss socialized medicine as public policy.

Leviathan Medicine, Leviathan Healthcare Insurance, Leviathan Union, Leviathan Big Government, and Leviathan Pharmaceutical all benefit from socialized medicine. As we have repeatedly emphasized in this book, public policies have a reason (the truth) and a rationale (the lie). The rationale for socialized medicine is that it helps patients (the lie). The reason for socialized medicine is that it helps the healthcare providers (the truth) and it provides life and more life for Leviathan (money and power).

For those who would quibble about the phrase "socialized medicine," consider that medicine, medical equipment and supplies, and the pharmaceutical industry are the most regulated industries in America. State governments license physicians, nurses, and pharmacists. Federal Governments have multiple agencies that monitor and regulate healthcare, such as the Centers for Disease Control and Prevention (CDC), the United State Food and Drug Administration (FDA), United States Department of Health and Human Services (HHS), Center for Medicare and Medicaid Services (CMS), the United States Drug Enforcement Administration (DNA), and the National Institutes of Health (NIH) among others. So whether we say healthcare is "socialized" or "highly regulated and controlled" does not matter. Leviathan has medicine by the throat no matter what the label.

While there are legitimate functions of government (police, courts, and national defense), most government action on the federal, state, and local levels targets economic activity. The beneficiaries of this targeting are various constituencies of Leviathan.

We mentioned above the economic rule pertaining to the supply-demand-price relationship. Let us consider how Leviathan Big Government tinkers with these components of economics in the healthcare industry to benefit its constituencies. Remember, it is highly advantageous to Leviathan that we not understand economics. If we understood economics, we could clearly see what Leviathan is doing and why.

Tinkering with Demand

The beneficiaries of Obamacare are healthcare insurance companies and providers of medical services. Why, otherwise, would the American Association of Retired Persons (AARP) and numerous other healthcare insurers have supported Obamacare?

Healthcare insurance companies benefit by Obamacare because **demand** for its products is mandated. Leviathan Big Government intervenes in the supply-demand-price relationship by increasing **demand** for the product (healthcare insurance) to the theoretical maximum. Practically everybody must have healthcare insurance or pay a fine.

Not everyone needs healthcare insurance. No one needs one-size-fits-all healthcare insurance. A young, healthy person has a property right in her own person and in her money. Leviathan Big Government violates property rights when it mandates that a person buy a product or service.

Shills for Leviathan will argue about the "free ride" that an uninsured person enjoys by not having healthcare insurance. The shill argues that when the uninsured person gets sick, then that person gets treatment at a hospital for which everyone else has to pay. That is true, but only in our presently socialized healthcare system. In a free-market economy, government is not in the business of bailing out people or enterprises when they make economic mistakes or miscalculations or suffer bad luck. In a free-market economy, the uninsured person will pay out of pocket for his unanticipated healthcare, he will enjoy the charity of others to provide the healthcare, or he will go without treatment. He will not be bailed out by government. Any thoughtful adult would have catastrophic healthcare coverage in a free-market economy.

Another intervention by Leviathan Big Government on the **demand** side is the requirement to have vaccines. In order to attend school, children are required to have dozens of vaccines. Most parents do not question Leviathan CDC's edict. Today, one in forty-two boys is diagnosed with autism spectrum disorder. Leviathan CDC assures us that the vaccine schedule is not implicated in this terrible epidemic.

Just think of how many visits to the pediatrician are necessitated in order to comply with the Leviathan CDC's recommended vaccine schedule. Parental compliance with Leviathan CDC's vaccine schedule accounts for most healthy-baby doctor visits.

Now that is as simple as simple can be: legally mandated **demand** helps Leviathan and its constituencies and hurts the consumer.

Tinkering with Price

Accidentally, the author discovered the price of his autistic son's seizure medicine. On the occasion of the last reorder, a $950 charge from the healthcare provider appeared on the credit card bill. A telephone call revealed that the provider overlooked the fact of insurance and a $920 credit was promptly issued. Three months' worth of generic seizure medication actually costs $950! The apparent cost to the customer is only the thirty-dollar deductible. Thirty dollars per three months to cure seizures is a trivial expense. Nine hundred and fifty dollars to cure seizures is not trivial, though it might be necessary. One can be sure, though, that a middle-class consumer of medical services will look for a lower-priced product or substitute products, or consider doing without, at the price of $950 per three months. (An online search reveals that this medicine is available from a Mexican pharmacy for $82 per three months. The American price is 11.6 times the Mexican price.[35]) Leviathan does not want customers shopping for better deals. Shopping is not good for Leviathan and its constituencies, the healthcare insurance companies and the medical service providers. Leviathan's constituencies prefer stability. They want to keep their customers.

Medical service providers include doctors, nurses, hospitals, pharmacists, and so on. There are dozens of professions includable under the name "medical service providers." To the theoretical delight of all of them, universal healthcare insurance means that the medical service providers will be paid. Not only will they be paid, but they will be paid by a third-party, Leviathan Healthcare Insurance, and not by the customer who would flyspeck the bill for high charges, overcharges, and errors. Paying customers also shop for alternatives to error-prone or high-priced medical service providers.

Now that is as simple as simple can be: legally mandated deep-pocket, disinterested payment for services at the hoped-for **price** benefits Leviathan and its constituencies and hurts the customer.

Tinkering with Supply

Now we tread on some doctor toes.

Professional Licensing

The author is a member of the governing body of a state-licensed professional group. An oft-discussed topic is competition by unlicensed people or organizations. Professional licensing has one purpose and one purpose only: to limit the *supply* of the service in order to impact the supply-demand-price relationship. Leviathan Big Government licenses entities in order to limit the *supply* of competitors for its constituencies.

The rationale (the lie) for licensing is to protect the customers. The reason (the truth) for licensing is to protect the entrenched and licensed service providers. Consider the hysterical and irrational opposition to Uber, the ride-sharing service, in various jurisdictions, including Paris, France. Consider the hysterical and irrational opposition to Airbnb.com, the house-sharing service in large cities, like New York City. The one and only reason for opposition to these services is the protection of licensed taxicab drivers in the case of Uber and large hotels in the case of Airbnb.

Now here comes the pain. Licensing in *all* professions has the same rationale: to protect the customers (the lie), and the same reason: to protect the entrenched and licensed service providers (the truth). ***The purpose of professional licensing is to suppress the supply of competing professionals.***

Good medical diagnosticians are vital, a matter of life and death. Good pharmacists are vital, a matter of life and death. Good lawyers are important, but rarely a matter of life and death. Good automobile diagnosticians are useful, a matter of hundreds of dollars. A good hairdresser is nice, but the matter is trivial, three weeks of hair growth will correct most errors, other than a total blue dye. Each of these occupations is licensed in all or some jurisdictions.

The presence of a federal, state, or local license does not guarantee that one is being served by a good doctor, a good lawyer, and so on. Everybody knows this fact, and sometimes people carefully shop for their professionals. More usual in this day and time is that customers, being locked into an employer-paid healthcare insurance plan, simply go to the doctor authorized by their insurer on the assumption that the healthcare insurer has carefully vetted the doctor.

Medical Care in the Absence of Licensing

Imagine a world in which medical services are delivered without interference by Leviathan Big Government. Example: Your child has a sore throat. Most parents and grandparents know that strep throat is one possible diagnosis in case of a sore throat. In our imaginary free society, the parent buys a strep test kit for less than five dollars at the local drugstore, over-the-counter and without a prescription. The kit tests "positive" for strep. Most parents know that penicillin by injection is the treatment of choice for strep. The approved 2016 price in Massachusetts[36] for a penicillin injection is $200. In a free market, the cost of a penicillin injection would be less than a Happy Meal. The cost in Mexico of penicillin is less than ten dollars. Penicillin sold for pets on the Internet costs ten or twenty dollars.[37] In our imaginary free society, the parent goes to the drugstore, buys the penicillin and the syringe, over-the-counter and without a prescription. The parent injects the child. Two days later the child is symptom free, cured of strep throat. Bottom line: In a free society, the child with strep would be cured by her parents in two days for about ten dollars, less than one-half of the co-pay on most insurance today. In today's world, Leviathan Healthcare Insurance pays the doctor upward of $200 for these services, twenty times the free-market price.

In a free-market economy, most pediatricians would be out of business. Some great pediatric diagnosticians would still be needed for exotic illnesses.

Doing away with state-mandated licensing for doctors will not happen in our lifetimes. Doctors, because of the high esteem in which they are held by the public, will continue to enjoy their government monopoly for as long as we shall live. What *will* happen is this: **Doctors will be replaced by the Internet.** Licensing will no longer limit the supply of medical services, and the cost of medical services will go down as a result.

Self-Help Medicine

On wrists everywhere these days are biometric bands that record physical location, movement, blood pressure, pulse, skin temperature, and blood oxygen. Home-use devices exist that draw blood and report blood sugar levels. Today, we can order without a prescription dozens of tests for various medical conditions on the Internet. One such online service is DirectLabs.com. Also, available today are numerous websites through which one can talk directly to a doctor. The Internet doctor, using testing she or the customer has ordered, can diagnose the condition or order treatment. While such a doctor will be licensed, the Internet availability of all doctors who chose to make themselves available, will greatly increase the supply of medical service providers. No longer will we be limited to doctors within a reasonable driving distance.

Now that is as simple as simple can be: legally suppressing *supply* by licensing service providers benefits Leviathan and its constituencies and hurts the customer.

Free-Market Health Insurance

World War II Origin

Employer-paid healthcare insurance is a consequence of government action during World War II. In order to ward off inflation, the government imposed wage-price controls. Labor groups objected. A government compromise exempted employer-paid healthcare insurance from the controls. Voila! Today, we have employer-paid, tax exempt healthcare insurance. In a free-market economy, there would be no tax incentive for employer-paid healthcare insurance. While employers would be free to offer it, employee-paid insurance is a better choice for the employee as employee-paid insurance is portable. An employee does not have to change automobile insurance carriers when he quits his job and goes to a new one. An employee does have to change healthcare providers in the event of a move under the current system. The lack of portability of employer-paid healthcare insurance is one of several strings that tie an employee to his employer. Limiting consumer choice is a major benefit for the constituencies of Leviathan. The ease of movement from one job to another by employees is definitely not something desired by employers.

Routine Services Are Not Insurable

Healthcare insurance should not cover regular physicals, well-baby checkups, teeth cleanings or eye sight checkups. These medical, dental, and vision services are not risks; they are routine human maintenance. The costs must simply be paid every year. When these noninsurable items are included in Leviathan Healthcare Insurance's policy, the customer's "insurance" premium must include a charge for these routine items embedded within the annual premium. Leviathan benefits by controlling the insured's money (life and more life for Leviathan, money and power). Leviathan Healthcare Insurance benefits by having prepayments for routine expenses under its control, prepayments that may never be used by the customer. Leviathan Medicine benefits by having the ***price*** of routine care ***hidden*** in an insurance premium, thus increasing ***demand*** for doctors and dentists with guaranteed payment of the ***price***.

An analogy to automobile insurance may reinforce this point. Automobile insurance does not pay for oil changes or replacement tires. Routine automobile maintenance is not a "risk." It is a certainty.

Neither the cost of routine maintenance for automobiles nor the cost of routine healthcare are insurable.

Imminent Risks Are Not Insurable

Insurance is a financial product the spreads a known, but not imminent, risk, such as fire, accident, death, or catastrophic illness, over a large number of people who are willing to share the risk by payment of an insurance premium. The insurance company manages the money paid as insurance premiums and pays claims according to the agreements of the premium payers. The limitation "imminent" is important because the insureds do not want to pay a death benefit for someone who has a life expectancy of three months. Insureds do not want to pay to rebuild a house that is already in flames. Insureds to not want to pay for a lifetime of healthcare for a person just diagnosed with a serious chronic illness. (The "preexisting condition" mandate of Obamacare overrules this usual requirement—nonimminent risk—of true insurance, turning healthcare insurance into a welfare scheme.)

Repealing Obamacare

A current mantra is "Repeal and replace Obamacare." There is no need to replace Obamacare. By eliminating the taxes, the regulations, and the government-imposed monopolies that currently hamper healthcare, healthcare would be efficient and inexpensive. We have shown that in a free economy, simple illnesses could be self-managed by application of general knowledge (our strep throat example). We have shown that in a free economy, regular physicals, well-baby checkups, teeth cleanings and eye sight checkups would simply be paid out-of-pocket by the customer, rather than by having the *price* for routine service hidden in an annual "insurance" premium. We have shown that in America drugs cost ten or twenty times what they cost in other parts of the world. In a free-market economy, these costs will decline even further.

In a free-market economy, healthcare would be no more problematical than buying a hamburger or a pair of shoes. Unexpected catastrophic healthcare costs would be paid by low-cost, multi-state, catastrophic insurance policies purchased by responsible individuals.

Demand for Great Doctors

Customers always need great medical diagnosticians, before, during, and after socialized medicine. Great doctors **do not need** Leviathan to spike *demand* for their services. Great doctors are always in demand and will always be highly compensated for their services, as they should be. In a free-market economy, high *prices* signal to the market (customers of medical services and suppliers of medical services) that *demand* is relatively high and *supply* is relatively low. Just like the entrepreneurs who drive electric generators to hurricane stricken cities, so too medical students and doctors will be drawn to the practice area in which *prices* are high. *Supply* of medical providers will rise in response to the spike in *prices* and *prices* will go down as more *supply* (doctors, researchers, entrepreneurs) move into the high-priced practice area.

In a free-market economy, the world will be swarming with great doctors. Discoveries and medical breakthroughs will come fast and furiously. Standards of living will rise. People worldwide will benefit.

In a free-market economy, customers will buy catastrophic healthcare insurance at low cost from hundreds of providers across state lines. No longer will customers be limited to purchasing healthcare insurance regulated by their home state. Routine medical expenses will be paid out of pocket. Those few people who fail to insure themselves and who lose their bet by suffering a terrible accident or by falling ill with a chronic or life-threatening illness will pay for that mistake from their savings, with the help of family or friends, or with the help of the millions of generous people in America including thousands of healthcare providers. There is no need for Leviathan Big Government's welfare state.

All the problems with healthcare today are caused by Leviathan. The problems will evaporate once we have pried the deadly fingers of Leviathan from the throat of the healthcare industry.

Doctoring: An Honorable Profession

"The first thing we do, let's kill all the lawyers" (Shakespeare, *Henry VI*, Part 2, Act 4, Scene 2). Lawyers can take a joke. The author is a lawyer. Doctors, not so much. Doctors, we fear, may take deep offense at this section. So let us repair the damage.

Doctoring is ***the*** most honorable profession. We all need doctors and are thankful for them. Many people worship their doctors and that worship is often justified. Doctors can and do perform miracles. Doctors deserve to be paid. Thank you, doctors.

On the other hand, doctors do not deserve to have Leviathan Big Government establish monopolies for them. A monopoly is a government mandate that only the grantee of the monopoly is allowed to perform the government-protected service or enter the government-protected contract. That government mandate is **naked force** that forbids willing parties from trading with one another. The government mandate is a violation of property rights. In effect, every licensed doctor has at his side a government thug pointing a gun at the head of the patient who would dare to ask an unlicensed doctor for medical advice or treatment. Doctors and citizens in general do not think in these terms (force and guns) because they are the subjects of Leviathan. We do not propose to change minds on this subject before the end of our one-hundred-years struggle to restore American Freedom.

The Great Recession/Depression

The Cause of Recessions

The biggest economic event is a depression or recession. A recession is a period of reduced economic activity. A depression is a longer period of seriously reduced economic activity. We will show in this section that the Great Recession, ongoing as we write, is caused by America's oligarchic government. A few examples will help us to understand how a period of reduced economic activity might come to pass.

A Local Depression

Many years ago, the author was the public administrator for a deceased person's estate. A public administrator is necessary when there is no family member or other interested party to windup the affairs of a dead person. The decedent in this case had never filed an income tax return, yet he had recently purchased a brand-new three-bedroom, two-bath house in a nice neighborhood for $200,000. The decedent's home was fully furnished. The house had a 100 percent mortgage on it and had been purchased with no down payment. The decedent owned a brand-new SUV. The car was 100 percent financed. The decedent had no money. The car was repossessed and the house foreclosed. How could this be? Prior to the onset of the current Great Recession, Leviathan Big Government was pushing the sale of houses to people who could not afford them.[38] Leviathan Big Government was successful and many houses were built. The houses were purchased with 100 percent financing by people who had no hope of paying for them. Today, the county of the decedent has the worst real estate market in the country with most houses significantly "underwater," meaning that the current fair market value of the house is less than the amount currently owed on the mortgage. The value of houses today in this county is less than one-half of the value before at the housing bubble burst (from 2007 to 2009). Home building remains seriously depressed.

China's Coming Depression

Another similar example comes from China today. The reader may have heard of China's ghost cities. China's Leviathan Big Government thought that it would be a good idea to build entire cities, not just subdivisions, despite the absence of real-world demand. The cities were built *in anticipation* of demand. In order to do this, China took money from its citizens by way of taxes and redirected the taxpayers' money to uses other than uses that would have been chosen by the taxpayers. Another method of financing China's ghost cities is simply to print money to pay for the building. Imagine the economic activity associated with building entire cities: massive employment, substantial purchases for services and supplies, and increased tax revenue for the government! China has been famous for its booming economy, and **demand**-side economic intervention like this is why. Unfortunately, nobody wants or needs to live in those cities. Thus, today China has many ghost cities. China's economy is now tanking, going into recession or depression.

As we can see by these two examples, recessions and depressions are caused by misallocation of resources, usually by government.

Subsidizing Depressions

Leviathan Big Government also aggravates recessions and depressions by prolonging them. When an individual makes an economic mistake, he suffers the consequence. For example, in the old days before Obamacare, if a young person gambled by failing to buy catastrophic healthcare insurance and then suffered terrible accident, he might have to declare bankruptcy being unable to pay enormous medical bills after treatment. The young person experiences shame and short-term loss. Relieved of the debt, the young person gets on with his life. The service providers, whose worthless claims were nullified by bankruptcy, write off their losses and get on with business. When a superorganism is threatened with such a loss, Leviathan Big Government might simply step in and buy the debt. Thus, we have the phrase in American economic lingo "too big to fail," usually referring to big banks. Leviathan Bank X buys or makes too many bad loans, such as home mortgages made by people who could not afford to pay them back. In a free market, too many bad loans results in the Leviathan Bank X going bankrupt. Leviathan Big Government, though, can buy the bad loans from Leviathan Bank X, replacing the worthless assets with taxpayers' cash, thus saving the bank from bankruptcy. The claims of the bad mortgages continue to exist in Leviathan Big Government's inventory of worthless assets.

A major activity of Leviathan Big Government is economic intervention to support the price of worthless assets for the benefit of many superorganisms.

Unfunded Government Pensions

Detroit, Michigan, and Stockton, California, have declared bankruptcy. Other American cities are bankrupt. Puerto Rico is bankrupt. Greece is bankrupt. (America is bankrupt, too. We just do not know it yet.) These Leviathan Big Governments are bankrupt for a reason: governments pay former employees who do not work.

The first rule of household management is that ***expenditures must be kept within the limits of income***. Leviathan Big Government violates this rule constantly.

A "crime" is a violation of a statute. Therefore, one cannot say that Leviathan Big Government's practice of granting, often in collusion with Leviathan Union, unfunded pensions to employees is a "crime." **One can say**, though, that if a corporation granted pensions to employees and failed to fund them, the corporation and its officers would be committing a serious federal crime. The Employee Retirement Income Security Act of 1974 (ERISA) has detailed rules for the funding of private retirement plans.

In order to please Leviathan Union and the public employees, Leviathan Big Government grants to its unionized employees pensions payable after the employee retires. Any normal person would realize that the promise to pay money in the future has a present cash value and once the promise is made, the present cash value should be set aside in a fund to pay the future claim. Every government official and every government finance employee knows this economic fact. However, elected officials have only a limited time in office. Because the consequences for creating unfunded liabilities will occur in the future, current elected officials know that they, personally, will not be held accountable for their failure to fund Leviathan Big Government's promises. Such behavior is immoral, corrupt, and as common as the sunrise.

Social Security is the same thing. American workers have paid into Social Security for their entire working lives. The payments by the employee and the matching payments by the employer have been spent by Leviathan Big Government, though Leviathan Big Government pumps propaganda constantly to deny the fact.[39] There is no Social Security trust fund.[40] The so-called trust funds are invested in United States Treasuries, backed by the full faith and credit of the United States government. These "investments" are simply IOUs, intragovernmental agency debt. What this means, simply, is that Leviathan Big Government in the future will extract more funds from taxpayers to pay the face value of the government securities when they are redeemed. An alternative "payment" scheme commonly used by Leviathan Big Government is to inflate the currency so that repayments are made in devalued dollars. In 2016, the recognized national debt is in the vicinity of $19 trillion. Some claim that when unfunded liabilities are considered our national debt exceeds $100 trillion. Of course, neither debt amount will ever be paid back, so what difference does it make if the "true" debt is $19 or $100 trillion or more? None.

The question is: What happens to America when the music stops? Unlike Detroit, America cannot file for bankruptcy.

Leviathan's Cost Interventions

As we have shown above, Leviathan affects economic activity by interfering with **supply**, **demand**, and **price**. Not yet mentioned is Leviathan's meddling with **costs** associated with creating **supply**, that is, with producing the product or providing the service. Leviathan Big Government intervenes to affect these **costs** for the benefit of Leviathan and its constituencies.

In order to protect Leviathan Big Pharmaceutical, Leviathan Big Government created the vaccine court. The National Childhood Vaccine Injury Act of 1986 (42 USC §§ 300aa-34) protects pharmaceutical companies from liability to customers for vaccine-caused injuries. The defendants are represented by government lawyers (United States Attorneys) and the claims are paid by the government. This massive intervention by Leviathan Big Government in favor of Leviathan Big Pharmaceutical reduces for this special constituent one of the usual *costs* associated with creating a product (the *supply*). A usual *cost* is *liability* for defective products.

In order to protect Leviathan Big Airline, Leviathan Big Government created the United States Transportation Security Administration (TSA) in response to the attacks on the World Trade Center and the Pentagon on September 11, 2001. The airlines were faced with financial ruin from lawsuits. In order to save them, Leviathan Big Government passed the Aviation and Transportation Security Act of 2001. Airline security, a *cost* of doing business, was taken over by Leviathan Big Government. Most people are persuaded that only Leviathan Big Government can provide security for Leviathan Big Airline.

A one-size-fits-all solution is always the preferred choice of Leviathan. Other examples of one-size-fits-all solutions include Obamacare and the Common Core State Standards Initiative (usually called simply "Common Core"). "Common Core" is an enormous project intended to nationalize public education to benefit Leviathan Education and Leviathan Book Publisher.

The massive intervention by Leviathan Big Government in favor of Leviathan Big Airline reduces one of the usual *costs* associated with providing a service (the *supply*). That usual *cost* is *liability* to passengers for failing to provide adequate security.

American Oligarchy

Leviathan Big Government's main job is to make interventions in the economy to benefit its constituencies. Leviathan Big Government's constituents are various oligarchs also known as Leviathan Union, Leviathan Big Business, and so on.

As we have said, there are legitimate government functions: the police, the courts, and national defense. These activities **do not** require continuous legislative activity, yet we have, on the federal level, **continuous legislative and rule making activity.** All of that legislative and rule making activity—beyond the three legitimate functions of government—is designed to **influence economic activity** for the benefit of the superorganisms that control us.

America's oligarchic government is best understood as interactions on the largest scale among America's sociopathic superorganisms. Superorganisms work in harmony with one another, for the most part, to secure life and more life for themselves. Much of that work is massive economic interventions.

Plato's Cave; Neo's Red Pill

Plato's great Allegory of the Cave occurs at the beginning of Book VII of *The Republic* (514a-520a). We are asked to imagine an underground cave in which men are chained in such a way that they can only look straight ahead at the rear wall of the cave. They cannot turn their heads to look at another. There is an opening behind them through which light from a fire passes. Between the fire and the backs of the prisoners is a stage onto which human handlers dance statues of men and animals and all sorts of things. The knowledge of the chained men is limited to the shadows dancing on the wall and the echoes. The puppets themselves are merely distorted representations. What would happen to a prisoner if he escaped, stood up, turned around to look into the fire, and saw the puppets and the puppet masters? Imagine that the escaped prisoner actually goes up and out of the cave into broad sunlight. What would happen to the escaped prisoner if he returned to the cave and tried to explain the things he has seen to the men still in chains. Would he be believed?

The 1999 film *The Matrix* tells the story of a fantastic world in which human beings are plugged into life supporting machines and are fed mental images by a malevolent computer program. The human beings are completely unaware of their status as slaves. The hero, Neo, is given the opportunity to escape the imaginary machine-created world and see the world as it really is. Neo takes the Red Pill to effect a change in his vision. Neo's mission becomes to set an enslaved humanity free from its machine masters.

Leviathan exists. Sociopathic superorganisms exist. They are all around us. They affect us in every way imaginable. We are educated by Leviathan Education. We are governed by Leviathan Big Government. We are informed by Leviathan Mainstream Media. We are propagandized by Leviathan Advertising. We are provided services by Leviathan Insurance, Leviathan Healthcare, Leviathan Union, and Leviathan Big Business. There is no area of our lives that is not substantially controlled by Leviathan.

Plato's Allegory of the Cave and *The Matrix* only slightly overstate the reality of our own circumstances.

Conclusion on Economics

Economics is simple. The first rule is that ***expenses must be kept within the limits of income***. The second rule is that there is a relationship among ***supply***, ***demand***, and ***price***. The third rule is that there are ***costs*** associated with producing ***supply***, whether that ***supply*** is a product or a service.

The legitimate functions of government are the police, the courts, and national defense. These legitimate activities require almost no ongoing legislation or rulemaking as that work once done is done. The legislature need ***not*** redraft the law punishing murder ***each year***. The only legitimate legislating that must be done on a regular basis is ***budgeting*** for legitimate government functions: police, courts, and national defense. If this is all Leviathan Big Government did, Washington, D.C., would be a very small town, rather than the seventh-largest metropolitan statistical area in the country.

Leviathan benefits when we believe that economics is complex. Leviathan benefits when we believe that we are too stupid to understand economics.

We must break our chains. We must look around us. We must see the puppet masters and their puppets. We must learn the puppet masters' purposes. We must go up, out of the cave, and into the light. We must take Neo's Red Pill.[41] The knowledge of economics provided by this chapter will help.

Then, Fabian Libertarians must ***educate others*** to see what is now so obvious to us: Most government action is massive intervention into the economy for the benefit of Leviathan and Leviathan's constituencies.

Chapter 4—The Little People

Leviathan has a rationale (the lie) for its existence and a reason (the truth). Most people only know the rationale (the lie). A good person, and most people are good, could not support Leviathan if she knew the truth. She needs to be deluded by Leviathan (first Leviathan Education, then Leviathan Media, and finally, Leviathan Big Government) into believing that she is supporting the good and acting morally. She is mistaken.

Leviathan's rationale (the lie) is usually some form of "**Save the children!**" The "children" can be any group of alleged incompetents who, according to Leviathan, cannot on their own achieve the end of Leviathan's government program and, therefore, need the assistance of Leviathan. The general term for "the children" is the title of this chapter "The Little People."

The Three Languages of Politics

Arnold Kling, in his 2013 e-book entitled *The Three Languages of Politics*, postulates that political groups use different descriptive words to talk and think about political issues. Libertarians evaluate issues along a ***freedom/coercion*** axis. Progressives use an ***oppressor/oppressed*** axis. Conservatives prefer a ***civilization/barbarism*** axis. So, for example, on the issue of the minimum wage, a Progressive sees an hourly laborer in China who is paid one dollar per hour as ***oppressed***. The employer is the ***oppressor***. A Libertarian sees a Chinese employee and employer who enjoy the ***freedom*** to contract or not. A government-imposed minimum wage, according to the Libertarian, is an act of ***coercion*** on both employer and employee. The Conservative favors government intervention via a minimum wage on the grounds that *civilization* is threatened by the *barbarism* of an hourly wage as low as one dollar.

Arnold Kling's axes help to understand "The Little People" idea of this chapter. "The Little People" are the "*oppressed*" people of the Progressive lexicon. "The Little People" are the "*barbarians*" of the Conservative lexicon. Progressives and Conservatives require the existence of "The Little People" in order to sustain their arguments in support of Leviathan Big Government.

"The Little People" Need . . . Whatever

Progressives believe that the many government programs are required to meet the needs of "The Little People." Progressives endorse the following statements: Children need government-provided elementary and secondary education. College students need government-provided student loans. Unemployed people need government-provided unemployment benefits. Poor people need government-provided welfare. Poor people need government-provided housing. Old people need government-provided retirement benefits. Sick people need government-provided socialized medicine. Air travelers need government-provided airline security. Farmers need government-provided price supports. Americans need government-provided financial support for the arts. Americans need government-provided parks and recreation. Americans need government-provided clean air and water.[42] Americans need government-provided safe food and drugs.

Libertarians agree that the following are good things:

- Elementary and secondary education;
- College education;
- The absence of unemployment and the pleasure of a job;
- A house to live in;
- Retirement income;
- Farm produce;
- Healthcare;
- Airline security;
- The arts;
- Parks and recreational areas;

- Clean air and water; and,
- Safe food and drugs.

Libertarians disagree with Progressives and Conservatives that such "goods" need be or should be provided by the government. The Progressive argument taken to an extreme leads to Democratic Totalitarianism. Democratic totalitarianism is, in fact, where we are heading. The Progressive argument goes like this: "X is good. The Little People need X. The Little People cannot get X without government assistance. Therefore, the government must supply "X." "X" can be anything, and will soon be *everything*.

Especially Needy People Do Exist

Libertarians admit to the existence of one category of "The Little People." There are, indeed, some especially needy people. For example, the author's adult son is severely autistic, without speech and in diapers. He cannot follow simple instructions and requires 24/7 one-on-one supervision. He is an *especially* needy person. He is, however, the responsibility of his parents. The most pressing concern for parents of an autistic child is the near certainty that the child will outlive his loving, caregiving parents. What will happen then? Sometimes, as in the present case, there is a loving, caring sibling who will assume the duties of caregiver once the parents are dead.

Libertarians do not advocate government programs even for especially needy people. Libertarians advocate families, moral communities, and charities caring for especially needy people. Americans are the most generous people on earth, and wealthy Americans are the most generous of all Americans. Needy people in American would be well cared for if the millions of Progressives and Conservatives (the majority of Americans) put their own money toward private charities rather than voting to *spend other people's money* on government welfare programs. In truth, we would not even need the money of Progressives and Conservatives to care for the needy if the Progressives and Conservatives would just *get off our backs*. We could care for the needy without them.

Progressives and Conservatives Believe Themselves "Superior"

Libertarians differ from Progressives and Conservatives in their belief, usually unstated, that the Progressive or the Conservative is *superior* to "The Little People." Progressives look out into the world and see "*oppressed*" people, from whom the Progressives are different. Conservatives look out into the world and see "*barbarians*," from whom the Conservatives are different. Libertarians look out into the world and see other "weird"[43] people, acknowledging that they themselves are "weird" too. Progressives want to "save" their "The Little People" from *oppression*. Conservatives want to "elevate" their "Little People" from *barbarism*. Libertarians just want to live and let live, wanting neither to "save" nor to "elevate" other independent, competent, and fully capable adults.

The impulse to judge other people by using oneself as the standard of value is endemic. Human beings have always identified "The Other." "The Other" is usually the enemy and, when possible, he is annihilated. A 10,000-year-old mass grave containing a murdered hunter-gatherer group was recently discovered in Kenya[44] suggesting that genocide predates agriculture. Perhaps as a consequence of *modern* Christianity (let us ignore The Crusades and the Thirty Years War), the American impulse toward "The Other" is no longer to kill him, but to "save" him from his "*oppressor*" or to "elevate" him from "*barbarism*." *The Libertarian impulse*, as we have said, *is to live and let live with others as peers.*

The "It's Force" Argument

Pure Libertarians always begin their arguments with Progressives and Conservatives about government programs by insisting (accurately) that all government programs are about "*force*." Whatever government program is being considered, it is funded by taxation which is the taking *by force* of taxpayers' money and redirecting that money to an expense not chosen by the taxpayer. For example, the government collects taxes and pays price supports to farmers. Furthermore, most government programs compel individuals, again

by force, to do or not to do something. For example, most employed people are required by the government to purchase healthcare insurance.

The "***it's force***" moral argument is **remarkably ineffective** with Progressives and Conservatives. The reason for this amazing fact is the Western cultural *meme* that all people in a democratic society are subject to the General Will (as articulated by Jean-Jacques Rousseau). The General Will is the will of all the people expressed through voting. We are free, according to Rousseau, when our will is in accord with the General Will. This idea is Democratic Totalitarianism. Isiah Berlin (1909–1997) famously said that Jean-Jacques Rousseau is "one of the most sinister and formidable enemies of liberty in the whole history of human thought." Most Americans believe that our essential freedom is the ***right to vote***, even when property rights are striped from us as a consequence of the vote. Since individual rights-striping government programs are a product of the General Will, we are "free" when we comply, according to Progressives and Conservatives. One suspects that this Western cultural *meme* is like an incurable virus in those infected. Progressives and Conservatives are not persuadable by the "***it's force***" moral argument. Young people do not usually begin adulthood infected. Because freedom will require immunizing young people against the pernicious doctrine of Rousseau's General Will, we will ***need*** one hundred years to restore American Freedom.

The Water Fountain Metaphor

As we suggested above, Progressives and Conservatives look out into the world and see "The Little People." When they do so, they are judging "The Little People" using themselves as the standard of moral value. The Progressive or Conservative judger is ***not*** the standard of moral value. Thinking about other individuals as separate, independent "fountains of value" will help us to discover the correct standard of moral value.

Compare an individual to a decorative water fountain. The Bellagio Fountains in Las Vegas, the Gardens of Versailles Fountain in France, the Trevi Fountain in Rome, and the Big Wild Goose Pagoda Music Fountain in Xian City, China, are examples of spectacular water fountains. There are millions of decorative water fountains in the world, mostly less spectacular than these examples.

Like a decorative water fountain, an able adult individual is an independent source of values. Fountains issue waters in beautiful sprays. Individuals issue values in dazzling arrays. The individual produces all the values that humans produce: children, food, shelter, clothing, objects of art, music, books, plays, operas, symphonies, computers, pride, families, friends, communities, nations, and so on. Any value one can conceive is produced by individuals. Some individuals are so productive that the zone of their output (like the shower from a great and brilliant fountain) benefits others outside their bounded zone. We enjoy the Bellagio Fountains from outside its bounded zone. A man like Bill Gates (1955–), founder of Microsoft, or a woman like Madame Curie (Polish/French scientist 1867–1934), who discovered radioactivity, shower values benefiting the entire world and posterity.

The Individual as Moral Center of the Universe

The individual is the center of the moral universe. The individual is the judge of her values. The *reason for being* of the individual is the pride she experiences in the values that she creates during her lifetime. She is the judge of her product. Hers is the only judgment that counts. The wholeness, harmony, and radiance of the individual are the ultimate values and these are the standards of value. *That which creates and sustains a beautiful adult human being is good.* That which inhibits, diminishes, or destroys a beautiful adult human being is evil.

We must recognize that each of us is our own beautiful value center. We are each the center of our own moral universe. In order for individuals to experience their *reason for being* (pride in productivity), they must be free to utilize their diverse capacities to flourish according to their own values, judgments, and abilities.

Progressive and Conservatives Are Not Gods

Progressives and Conservatives impose their own value judgments upon "The Little People." Like gods surveilling their domains, Progressives and Conservatives judge this or that individual as "good" (like them), "oppressed" (not like them), "barbarian" (not like them), or "bad" (not like them). Like an expert committee judging great water fountains in a worldwide contest, the Progressives and Conservatives judge the winners and losers among human beings, deciding who needs saving and who needs elevating. Progressives and Conservatives are not gods, though. They are simply water fountains among millions, like the rest of us. They have no high perch that entitles them to judge other water fountains and then to *interfere with them*. Any outside interference necessarily disrupts the life flow of the individual fountain of value.

Remember the list of "goods" from above:

- Elementary and secondary education;
- College education;
- The absence of unemployment and the presence of income;
- A house to live in;
- Retirement income;
- Farm produce;
- Healthcare;
- Airline security;
- The arts;
- Parks and recreational areas;
- Clean air and water; and,
- Safe food and drugs.

All of these "goods" are produced in a free society by the millions of independent individual family units (the water fountains) in accordance with their unique abilities, judgments, and values. Some values, like "the arts" (think of a production of the opera *La Bohème*), can only be produced by a collaboration of individuals, including Giacomo Puccini (Italian composer, 1858–1924), who, like Monsieur Bill Gates and Madame Curie, is a giant.

Leviathan Creates "The Little People"

Every government program contributes to the creation of "The Little People." Taxes take money from the individual producer and redirect the producer's income to the government's aims. This taking and redirection **diminishes the flourishing individual** from the perspective of his own fountain. The taking by force and redirection of private property is evil.

The denial by Leviathan Big Government of the right of an employee to a job on his own terms (including working for less than a minimum wage), creates an entire category of "The Little People," the unemployed and the unemployable. The denial by Leviathan Big Government of a person to work in any job she is capable of performing because she is unlicensed, contributes to the unemployed and unemployable category of "The Little People." The denial by Leviathan Big Government of a person to save for his retirement due to burdensome taxes, regulations, and restrictions on employment, creates an entire category of "The Little People," the poor elderly person who is dependent upon Leviathan Big Government for survival through welfare, public housing, and Social Security. The perverse incentives created by welfare programs discourage people from working, thus depriving them of the very meaning of life—pride in their productivity. Another perverse incentive of Leviathan Big Government's welfare system is the single-parent household. The lack of an intact family (father and mother present in the home with the children) greatly contributes to criminality, thus creating another category of "The Little People," physically and psychologically damaged children who become criminals.

As President Ronald Regan (1911–2004) once famously said, "Government is not the solution to our problem; government is the problem." **There is no major social problem today that is not caused by Leviathan Big Government.** Every Progressive and Conservative example of "The Little People" is the creation of Leviathan Big Government.

Conclusion

"The Little People" are the excuse of Progressives and Conservatives for all of their *meddling*. They justify to themselves disruption, intervention, regulation, restraint, harassment, terrorization, imprisonment, and murder (for example, wars waged to impose democracy), on the grounds that their intentions are good. The Progressives intend to "save" the "oppressed." The Conservatives intend to "elevate" the "barbarians." What the Progressives and Conservatives end up doing is wreaking havoc. "Cry 'Havoc!' and let slip the dogs of war."[45]

Libertarians do not believe in "The Little People." We are all more or less "weird." Libertarians desire peace. Libertarians desire liberty. Libertarians want to be left alone. Libertarians desire simply to live and let live in a free society where individual rights are protected by the rule of law.

Chapter 5—Whose Question Is It?

"We are all Socialists now." The Socialists have won and the job of Fabian Libertarians is to recover American Freedom. While it is impossible to convert the millions of existing adult American Socialists, maybe we can protect American young people from the pernicious American social *meme* heretofore discussed: the belief in Jean-Jacques Rousseau's General Will and the related consequence of Democratic Totalitarianism.

Libertarians are fully aware that "Mind your own business" is the shortest expression of the Libertarian political philosophy. This chapter introduces a new take on this ancient advice.

We all participate in debates about public questions from time to time. We dispute, for example, whether we ought to install mercury light bulbs, also called compact fluorescent light (CFL) bulbs. We argue about whether we ought to buy thirty-two-ounce Cokes in New York City. We argue about whether we take the flu shot. The list of so-called public questions is practically endless.

The new take on the ancient advice "Mind your own business" is the question "***Whose question is it?***" Questions have an *owner*, and the owner **has the right to answer her question** for herself.

The argument includes these points:

- An example is given in which Chinese dictator Mao Zedong imposes his scientific conclusions upon the Chinese people with terrible consequences.
- The idea of Scientism is explained. A dictatorship of science is evil.
- Most of us are little "o" objectivists, believing that there is only one right and true answer to every question. This belief does not entitle us to answer other peoples' questions.

- Some causes of the problem of "minding other people's business" are suggested: the public media and our complete lack of privacy.
- A brief explanation of natural law is provided showing that we all get it.
- Freedom is not the right to vote. Democratic totalitarianism is evil.
- The claim is made for a zone of privacy within which we all have ownership of certain questions, their answers, and the consequences.

The Great Leap Forward

Mao Zedong was born on December 26, 1893, and died on September 9, 1976. He is commonly referred to as Chairman Mao. Chairman Mao was the founding father of the People's Republic of China, and held power from October 1, 1949, until his death in 1976. Chairman Mao presided over an economic and social program called the Great Leap Forward from 1958 to 1961.

Among the programs of the Great Leap Forward was an agricultural technique called Deep Plowing. Deep plowing was a scientific theory of Soviet biologist Trofim Lysenko (1898–1976). Scientific dissent from Lysenko's theories was outlawed in 1948 in the Soviet Union and dissenters from Lysenko's theories were purged from their positions and many were imprisoned. People in America today get purged from their positions by taking heretical positions. (Dare any American public scientist today suggest that "global warming" or "climate change" is in the slightest detail questionable?) Deep plowing, up to two meters deep, was thought to improve crop yield.

There were many aspects to the Great Leap Forward beyond Deep Plowing, but the ultimate result of the Great Leap Forward was that between eighteen and forty-five million people died from starvation caused by crop failure or were killed by the government outright when they resisted the programs of the Great Leap Forward.

The problem with the Great Leap Forward is not that the totalitarian government was wrong in its scientific opinion that deep plowing would help crop yield. The problem is that ***it is wrong for***

the government to impose its scientific opinions on its people. The question—How should I grow my wheat or my rice?—does not belong to the government. The question—How should I grow my wheat or my rice?—belongs to the individual farmer.

Scientism

Scientism is the religion of science. The term includes people who would impose their scientific conclusions on others. People under the spell of scientism will argue that their scientific conclusions ought to be imposed upon others because they think people are dumb. Chairman Mao held that Lysenko's scientific conclusion—Deep Plowing is great for crop yield—was true. Chairman Mao held that people are dumb. Therefore, for their own sake, Mao imposed his "science" upon the people.

The only difference between Chairman Mao's view and, say, Mayor Blumberg's view on thirty-two-ounce sodas in New York City (thirty-two-ounce sodas should be banned according to Blumberg), is that few people are likely to die from lack of corn-sugar-spiked fizzy water.

Quite a few of us think that our so-called "correct" scientific views ought to be imposed upon others. While we all have respect for science, not everyone is willing to permit a dictatorship of scientists. (Fabian Libertarians despise a dictatorship of science.) The conclusions of true science are always provisional. True science says that based upon the evidence thus far examined, we conclude to a reasonable certainty that "X," whatever "X" is, is true.

The ultimate responsibility for the life of the individual rests with the individual. The individual must make his own provisional conclusions based upon science or upon the authority of science, or upon his own experience, or upon the experience of others he trusts, or upon intuitions that he interprets as God-given or as mysteries from his subconscious, or upon whatever basis in his judgment he will live his life.

Lysenko's Deep Plowing conclusions, once thought true, turned out to be false. We have seen many such turns of scientific opinion in our own lifetimes.

Little "o" objectivists

Many readers are little "o" objectivists. Big "O" Objectivism is the philosophy of Ayn Rand and is one of the philosophical roots of Libertarianism. Little "o" objectivists are not, necessarily, the followers of Ayn Rand. Little "o" objectivists hold the view that there is one and only one *right* answer to every question. Most people in America will agree that there is only one *right* answer to every question.

- For example, is the world flat? There is only one correct answer.
- Is there a God? There is only one correct answer.
- Is it right to buy and drink a thirty-two-ounce soda infused with high fructose corn syrup in New York City?
- Is it right to buy and consume foie gras in California?
- Is it right to follow the Center for Disease Control's (CDC's) vaccine schedule?
- Is it right to put our eight-year-old autistic child in a group home?
- Is it right to allow your eight-year old girl child to participate in beauty contests?
- Is it right that an Amish family refuse CDC and government mandated vaccinations?
- Is it right to put your child in a private, secular school?
- Is it right to smoke marijuana?
- Is it right that to shop at Wal-Mart?
- Is it right to raise your child under Sharia law and teach her to hate America and to wear a burka?

Each of us has an answer to each of these questions and each of us has no doubt that we are right in our answers. **None of us has the same answer to all of these questions.** Small "o" objectivists believe that there is only one true and correct answer to all properly formed questions. Even though it is true that there is only one true and correct answer, it is not important what the "right" answer to the question is. **The real question is: "Whose question is it?**

"Should Mr. Smith shop at Wal-Mart?" is *Mr. Smith's* question. *Mr. Smith* has a right to insist upon this.

Why Are We Inclined to Meddle?

We might wonder why it is not obvious that *the important question* is: "Whose question is it?" Why are we all so quick to answer other people's questions? *Why are we willing to impose our answers to their questions on them?*

24/7 News Media

One reason is our public media. Many of us live in the news. We surf the Internet. We watch cable television. We listen to talk radio. We look over the shoulders of real people while observing them on reality television shows. *We have opinions about everyone else's questions.* We express those opinions during the show to our television watching mates. We want our opinions enacted.

No Privacy

Another reason is our now nearly complete lack of privacy. The National Security Agency (NSA) is recording all our telephone calls.[46] Many of us voluntarily report the smallest details of our lives on Facebook. We are constantly under the scrutiny of security cameras in stores, in banks, in public buildings, at stoplights, on most city streets, and by satellite from space. London may be the most security-camera-covered city today. But soon all major cities will have nearly total security camera coverage. The Federal Aviation Administration (FAA) is considering approving unmanned drones (the drones coming back from our many foreign wars) to spy on American citizens. The drones are, as yet, unarmed. But arming them is the next, very easy step. George Orwell's Big Brother is indeed watching us and he has a gun. *1984* has come to pass. In airports we are only one-step away from physical rectal and gynecological examinations. We are certain to have *electronic* rectal, gynecological, and body-interior scans very shortly. Nobody cares about this abuse. We routinely tolerate this **disgraceful humiliation**.

Because of our always-looking-over-the-shoulder media and our nearly complete lack of privacy, we are used to having opinions about other people's business.

Combine our habit of looking over other people's shoulders with our absolute faith in unbridled democracy, and we think that we as a democratic group have the right to assert **and enforce our opinions** about other people's business. Of course, this societal *meme* is Jean-Jacques Rousseau's General Will become **Democratic Totalitarianism**.

Mind Your Own Business

Plato's *Republic* asserts that the essence of justice is to "Mind your own business." Let us consider this moral proposition—**Mind your own business!**—for a few minutes.

Natural Law

There is such a thing as natural law. Most people think that they do not understand natural law. These days natural law is not taught. Everyone, though, experiences natural law. Natural law is a law that arises from human nature. We "feel" it as a part of our nature.

Here is a benign example of the feeling of natural law. Suppose you are a skilled guitar maker. You can make a guitar from scratch. You collect the wood and finish it. You buy the metal parts. You manufacture the strings and tuning studs. After months of hard work, you accomplish your task and you complete a great acoustic guitar. Your master work is a Stradivarius of guitars. This handmade guitar is yours. It is *your* guitar. If someone tried to take it from you, you would be mad and you would try to keep your guitar. ***This feeling is the natural right of property***.

Another example is your body. An ugly stranger comes up to you and pinches your butt, your breast, or your penis. You are furious. You hit him. You call the police. Your property interest in your body has been violated and you defend it. ***This feeling is the natural right***

of property. Adam Smith (Scottish moral philosopher, 1723–1790) said, "Every man has a property in his own person. This nobody has a right to, but himself."

Another example is your children. Another ugly stranger suddenly runs up to you and your child in the grocery store. He tries to snatch your child. You defend your child. You come close to killing the attacker to defend your child. ***This feeling is the natural right of property.***

All of these examples are instances of natural rights, natural property rights.

Note that your guitar, your behind, and your child are all a subset of you, your life. Life is the highest right and includes other rights such as your guitar, your behind, and your child. "Life, liberty, and the pursuit of happiness." The opening lines of the Declaration of Independence: "We hold these truths to be self-evident, that all men are created equal, that they are endowed by their Creator with certain unalienable Rights, that among these are Life, Liberty and the Pursuit of Happiness."

One need not be religious to assert the existence of natural rights. The sense of entitlement to these rights arises from your nature as a human being. Your sense of entitlement is shared by all other normally functioning adult human beings. Your sense of entitlement is enforced by laws in all human societies to a greater or lesser degree.

The right to property (life, liberty, the pursuit of happiness) is a natural right in this sense.

The Frog and the Boiling Pot

Our property rights—the rights to life, liberty, and the pursuit of happiness—are being whittled away. We are like the proverbial frog that sits in a pot of cool water over a fire and is not aware, until he is cooked, that the water has been brought to a deadly boil. Year by year we are slowing becoming boiled frogs.

Freedom Is Not the Right to Vote

We are taught that freedom is the right to vote. ***Freedom is not the right to vote***. The right to vote is one of several constitutional techniques intended to preserve freedom. The founding fathers were fully aware that the right to vote was only a technique and not a perfect one. That is why the founding fathers of America did not found a democracy, but rather a republic with three branches of government that shared limited powers. The Constitution, it was hoped, would limit the power of the government. The right to vote for our representatives and the president was merely one of several techniques to preserve freedom

Freedom is the societal condition in which property rights are protected by the rule of law. One can be completely free in a monarchy with no right to vote if one is the subject of a good monarch.

The moral measure of a society is on a scale that begins on one extreme with totalitarianism and ends on the other with fully protected property rights: life, liberty, and the pursuit of happiness.

In a free society, the zone of privacy is extensive. The zone of privacy is the area of life in which we each own all of our questions, the answers, and the consequences. In a totalitarian society, the zone of privacy is very small or nonexistent. In a totalitarian society, all or most of the questions, their answers, and the consequences belong to the State.

Review the Questions

Let us go over the moral questions listed above and try to categorize them.

- Is the world flat? The individual's answer has no meaningful consequences for others. The main consequence is that the person who says the world is flat is uneducated. Matters of personal scientific opinion are within the zone of privacy.
- Is there a God? The individual's answer has no meaningful consequences for others. In America we do not permit the imposition of a state religion. Matters of personal religious opinion are within the zone of privacy.

- Is it right to buy and drink a thirty-two-ounce soda infused with high-fructose corn syrup in New York City? The individual's answer has no meaningful consequences for others. That a person might become fat is not relevant to a free society where the society does not bear the burden of its members' bad choices. Matters of personal taste are within the zone of privacy.
- Is it right to buy and consume foie gras in California? The individual's answer has no meaningful consequences for others. Matters of personal taste are within the zone of privacy. The California ban on foie gras, effective July 1, 2012, was enacted in 2004. The law was enacted at the urging of various animal-rights groups. We acknowledge the existence of a marginal zone in this case. We would not tolerate the public torturing of house pets and would seek to intervene. Stuffing food into gooses is not the same as the torturing of animals. The creation and consumption of food always involves some discomfort *for the food*.
- Is it right to follow the CDC's vaccine schedule?
- Is it right that we put our eight-year-old autistic child in a group home?
- Is it right that you allow your eight-year-old girl child to participate in beauty contests?
- Is it right that an Amish family refuse CDC and government mandated vaccinations?
- Is it right that you raise your child in a private, secular school?

These last five questions are all questions pertaining to the raising of one's own children. The question of how people raise their children is within the zone of privacy. While these particular questions are within the zone of privacy, there are questions on the margin between private and public. For example, the right to use faith-healing for your deathly ill child is more difficult, and we will not resolve all marginal questions here. We merely acknowledge the existence of the margin. There are consequences beyond the individual parent in the case of faith-healing. In particular cases, the certain death of a child might be the result. In such a case, there are consequences for others, in particular, the soon-to-be-dead child.

- Is it right to smoke marijuana? The individual's answer has no meaningful consequences for others. Matters of personal taste are within the zone of privacy.
- Is it right that you shop at Wal-Mart? The individual's answer has no meaningful consequences for others. Matters of personal taste are within the zone of privacy.
- Is it right to raise your child under Sharia law and teach her to hate America and to wear a burka? The individual's answer has no meaningful consequences for others. Matters of personal religious taste are within the zone of privacy. Again, this question approaches, but does not cross, the border into a marginal area.

As can be seen, an important criterion for public and private questions is whether the answer has public consequences or only private consequences.

Conclusion

When debating and before your discussion becomes too hot, ask, "Whose question is it?" If the question does not **belong to you**, there is no reason for high emotion. It just does not matter. If a friend needs help with one of **her questions**, of course, you are free to help. But the question, the answer, and the consequences will always be hers.

The argument of this chapter has these points:

- China's Great Leap Forward, during which the Chinese government imposed its scientific opinion about Deep Plowing upon its subjects, resulted in the deaths of tens of millions.
- Scientism, the religion of science, inclines many to a dictatorship of science. A dictatorship of science is evil.
- Most of us are little "o" objectivists, believing that there is only one right and true answer to every question. This belief does *not* entitle us to answer other peoples' questions.
- Natural law exists and we all intuitively understand it.

- At least two causes of our meddling in the business of others exist: (1) our meddling public media, and, (2) our almost complete lack of privacy.
- The right to vote is not freedom. Freedom is the societal condition in which our property rights—the rights to life, liberty, and the pursuit of happiness—are protected by the rule of law.
- There exists a zone of privacy within which we all have ownership of certain questions, their answers, and the consequences of those answers.

Recognize that the important thing is **not** the **correct answer** to every question. ***The important thing is: Whose question is it?***
Please, mind your own business.

Chapter 6—The Plan: Act One

How are we to conduct our **one-hundred-years** effort to restore American Freedom? Let us look to our namesake, Quintus Fabius Maximus Cunctator (280–203 BC), for guidance.

Shortly after the Carthaginian general Hannibal (247–183 BC) crossed the Alps in 218 BC to invade Italy, he defeated a Roman army under the command of Consul Gaius Flaminius Nepos (–217 BC). Flaminius himself was killed in the Battle of Lake Trasimene in Tuscany. Fifteen thousand Roman soldiers were killed at Trasimene. When the citizens of Rome learned of this terrible defeat, they feared that Rome would soon be attacked and destroyed by Hannibal. Hannibal was only ninety miles due north of Rome. Fabius Maximus, a former consul sixty-three years old at this time, was elected dictator to take control in the emergency. Rather than rush to war, Fabius Maximus assured the people that Rome had not lost because Hannibal commanded a superior force, but rather because Flaminius failed to attend to important religious rites before assuming command. Fabius ordered the careful and fastidious performance of the rites.

Plutarch (45–120) tells us that these religious activities reassured the Romans that the gods were on their side. Fabius, though, had confidence in himself and his plans. While modern Americans have no common religious rituals to perform (because of our religious diversity), we might nonetheless gesture toward the example of Fabius by heeding the advice of Luke 6:42:

> Either how canst thou say to thy brother, Brother, let me pull out the mote that is in thine eye, when thou thyself beholdest not the beam that is in thine own eye? Thou hypocrite, cast out first the beam out of thine own eye, and then shalt thou see clearly to pull out the mote that is in thy brother's eye.

Carthaginian general Hannibal ravaged Italy from 218 BC until his recall to Carthage in 203 BC, a period of fifteen years. Fabius Maxius died shortly after the withdrawal of the Carthaginians. Hannibal did not die until twenty years after his recall at the age of sixty-four. In 183 BC Hannibal committed suicide because the Romans, still terrified of Hannibal, demanded the surrender of Hannibal and his country of exile, Bithynia, near modern-day Istanbul, consented to deliver him to Rome.

Look to Our Own Moral Characters

The plan of this book does not anticipate a full restoration of American Freedom for one hundred years. Few of us alive today will not see final victory. Therefore, in addition to fighting for freedom, we must resolve to live well. We must strive to live beautifully. To live beautifully is to live virtuously.

There are at least two benefits to living beautifully. The first benefit is that we will flourish and be happy in our time. The second benefit is that we will set a fine example for those we hope to persuade to join us in our struggle to restore American Freedom.

We have not always looked the part of beautiful human beings.

In 1972, the Georgia Libertarian Party held its first national convention in Atlanta, Georgia. Some of the attendees looked like characters from the iconic Star Wars bar scene. Ben Obi-Wan Kenobi said of the alien city where the Space Bar is located, "Mos Eisley spaceport: You will never find a more wretched hive of scum and villainy. We must be cautious." While all present (including the author) at the conference were certainly good and moral people, a conservative visitor might have doubted it from our scruffy, eclectic appearance.

The first element of our one-hundred-years plan is to appear and **to be beautiful**. A related ancient Greek concept is *arête*, meaning excellence of any kind or moral virtue. By definition, a beautiful and excellent human being is a **lady** or a **gentleman**.

Courage

Aristotle is America's philosopher. Without knowing it, most Americans are Aristotelians. We profess to live by Aristotle's logic. He is the Father of Science. His list of virtues is instantly recognizable: courage, temperance, generosity, magnificence, magnanimity, appetite for honor, gentleness, truthfulness, charm, friendliness, sense of shame, righteous indignation, and justice.

For Aristotle, virtues are means between two extremes—the famous **golden mean**. In the case of courage, the extremes are cowardice and rashness. Courage is Aristotle's paradigmatic virtue. The courage of which Aristotle speaks is the courage displayed in war, though analogies can be made to other domains of human action, like politics. The analogy to politics is apropos.

Politics is a "civilized" substitute for war. The goal of war is very frequently to acquire the property of others—territory, money, and natural resources, including human workers, i.e., slaves. The business of the United States Congress is almost entirely the acquisition and control of the property of others. See P. J. O'Rourke's 1991 book, *Parliament of Whores: A Lone Humorist Attempts to Explain the Entire U.S. Government*. Countries engage in war to seize the property of others or to protect their own property from being taken or to achieve glory or to avenge dishonor. Commonly countries engaging in war will cloak the **reason** for the war (the theft of property) with a plausible and appealing **rationale**, usually a humanitarian motive. Compare, for example, the 1994 Rwandan genocide in which the United States did **not** intervene with the 2011 Libyan intervention by the United States. In Rwanda, Hutu thugs killed between eight hundred thousand and one million Tutsis. The United States had no economic motive in Rwanda and, therefore, did not get involved, though humanitarian considerations were present in the extreme. The nonintervention in the 1994 Rwandan genocide **undermines** the humanitarian motive claimed for the Libyan intervention in 2011—"to prevent attacks on civilians." The true reasons for war are often a complex mixture of **power, pride**, and **property**. Rarely is the alleged humanitarian motive more than just a cover story.

The same is true for the "civilized" substitute for war—politics. **The goal of modern politics is to acquire the property of others**. The only difference between politics and war is one of means—in politics people are not usually killed. All other tools of war are used in politics. The word "civilized" is within quotes precisely because, while killing is not a usual tool of politics, spying, lying, personal attacks, family attacks, and bribery are. None of the tools of politics—spying, lying, personal attacks, family attacks, and bribery—is a civilized method. Note that Fabian Libertarians will ***not*** be using these usual tools of politics, though we will have to defend against them.

The Aristotelian virtue of courage will be a crucial virtue during our **one-hundred-years** effort to restore American Freedom. While we can anticipate vicious attacks by Leviathan's servants once the threat of Fabian Libertarianism is identified, careful planning will reduce our risk and bolster our **courage**.

An important characteristic of all of Aristotle's virtues is that there is no formula by which to judge an action courageous or temperate and so on. The judgment of a courageous act is ***in the perception*** of it. Therefore, if a soldier sees a hand grenade lobbed in among his patrol and he shields his brothers-in-arms from the explosion at the cost of his own life, his act might be ***perceived*** as a courageous act. The observer says, "That was a beautiful thing to do." While one might write paragraphs describing the act, no amount of prose can reproduce ***the perception*** of the beautiful act. On the other hand, poetry can evoke The Beautiful:

The Charge of the Light Brigade
by Alfred, Lord Tennyson, 1854

> Half a league half a league,
> Half a league onward,
> All in the valley of Death
> Rode the six hundred:
> 'Forward, the Light Brigade!
> Charge for the guns' he said:
> Into the valley of Death
> Rode the six hundred.

MARTIN COWEN

'Forward, the Light Brigade!'
Was there a man dismay'd?
Not tho' the soldier knew
  Some one had blunder'd:
  Theirs not to make reply,
  Theirs not to reason why,
  Theirs but to do and die,
  Into the valley of Death
    Rode the six hundred.

Cannon to right of them,
Cannon to left of them,
Cannon in front of them
  Volley'd and thunder'd;
Storm'd at with shot and shell,
Boldly they rode and well,
Into the jaws of Death,
Into the mouth of Hell
  Rode the six hundred.

Flash'd all their sabres bare,
Flash'd as they turn'd in air
Sabring the gunners there,
Charging an army while
  All the world wonder'd:
Plunged in the battery-smoke
Right thro' the line they broke;
  Cossack and Russian
Reel'd from the sabre-stroke,
  Shatter'd and sunder'd.
Then they rode back, but not
  Not the six hundred.

Cannon to right of them,
Cannon to left of them,
Cannon behind them
  Volley'd and thunder'd;
Storm'd at with shot and shell,

> While horse and hero fell,
> They that had fought so well
> Came thro' the jaws of Death,
> Back from the mouth of Hell,
> All that was left of them,
> Left of six hundred.
>
> When can their glory fade?
> O the wild charge they made!
> All the world wonder'd.
> Honour the charge they made!
> Honour the Light Brigade,
> Noble six hundred!

Temperance

Ladies and gentlemen are temperate. This virtue pertains mostly to certain pleasures like food, drink, and sex. The extremes are dissipation and insensitivity. Note that sensual pleasures are not foregone; they are simply enjoyed in moderate doses. Gluttons, alcoholics, and sex maniacs are not ladies and gentlemen. The extreme of insensitivity to pleasures is rare and might include ascetics or righteous teetotalers. Temperance is crucial to a happy life. Temperance is also a virtue that others especially look for in their leaders.

Generosity

The extremes of generosity are wastefulness and stinginess. This virtue is important because our enemy, Leviathan, uses the rationale (the lie) of **generosity** to justify its programs. Leviathan's reason (the truth) for all programs is life and more life for Leviathan, power and money. For example, the minimum wage is represented to be an act of **generosity**, when in fact the minimum wage creates a large group of unemployable people who need Leviathan's welfare programs, including socialized medicine. The minimum wage reduces the **supply** of potential employees, causing an increase in **demand** for the new, smaller pool, with a consequent increase in the *price* (wages and salaries).

Ladies and gentlemen are generous. One is generous with that which one produces. ***The meaning of life is the pride and pleasure that each of us enjoys in our productivity.*** Older people tend to be the most generous. Young adults are busy finding and exploiting their personal powers. They are building careers, families, and communities according to their unique abilities, tastes, and training. Young people trade their productivity for money and other goods. Beyond their trading, most young adults are, in fact, generous within their limited means. An older adult who has achieved and completed her career, who has raised her family, and who has built her communities, no longer needs to trade her productivity for money and other goods. She is free to lavish her productivity on the rest of us. The simple act of a retired lady working as a volunteer in a hospital is the paradigmatic act of generosity.

The act of becoming a Fabian Libertarian is itself an act of ***generosity.*** Few of us alive today will know the final success of our fight for American Freedom. We will, of course, experience pride and pleasure in our small successes in political action as they come. Freedom fighting is a notoriously unrewarding activity for the fighter. The benefits of our successful fight to restore American Freedom will flow to our children and grandchildren and to the rest of humankind.

Magnificence

The extremes of magnificence are gaudiness and chintziness. Magnificence is related to the virtue of generosity by degree. Magnificence is related to great things. Generosity is related to small things. Scottish-American industrialist Andrew Carnegie (1835–1919) famously used his enormous fortune to build three thousand public libraries and seven thousand church organs. He donated 90 percent of his fortune to charity. In our own time, Microsoft founder Bill Gates (1955–) is busy with his philanthropic works through the Bill & Melinda Gates Foundation. The foundation is interested in improving healthcare and in reducing poverty. Andrew Carnegie and Bill Gates are magnificent.

Fabian Libertarians hope to find magnificent ladies and gentlemen to help us restore American Freedom. Bill Gates does not know it, but the single greatest contribution to the reduction of world poverty that he might make is to teach the populations that interest him that ***freedom is the protection of property rights by the rule of law***. A majority of world countries have property rights severely curtailed by totalitarian governments. America did not become great because some magnificent ladies or gentlemen taught us to use flush toilets (one of the Gates Foundation programs). America became great because we were free. A mostly free America was the sine qua non for the self-made wealth of Andrew Carnegie and Bill Gates. ***Freedom precedes the wealth of the masses***.

Magnanimity

Greatness of soul is a virtue with which Americans are not very comfortable. The virtue is related to pride, one of the seven deadly sins: lust, gluttony, greed, sloth, wrath, envy, and ***pride***. Pride is not spoken well of in the *Bible*: "Charity suffereth long, *and* is kind; charity envieth not; charity vaunteth not itself, is not puffed up" (1 Corinthians 13:4). The ancient Greeks condemned excessive pride, which they called ***hubris***.

The extremes of magnanimity are vanity and smallness of soul. A great-souled person expects, and has a right to expect, honors for herself from the correct person, in the correct way and portion, at the correct time and place, and for the right reasons. The great British statesman Winston Churchill (1874–1965), whose leadership during the Second World War helped saved the world from the Nazis, was great-souled. Churchill was entitled to and received great honors for his virtues.

In Aristotle's theory a magnanimous person necessarily possesses all thirteen virtues. In a marvelous phrase, Aristotle says that it would not be fitting "for someone great-souled to run away with wildly swinging arms, or to be unjust."[47]

Fabian Libertarians will need great-souled individuals if we are to succeed.

Appetite for Honor

Appetite for honor (small) is related to magnanimity (great) in the same way that generosity (small) is related to magnificence (great). Not everyone can be a Winston Churchill. Everyone can, though, aspire to personal excellence within the range of her capacity. To the extent one achieves ordinary virtue, an appetite for honor is appropriate. Among the rewards for virtue is to be honored by others for one's achievements.

As we strive for personal excellence, we expect honors for ourselves from the correct person, in the correct way and portion, at the correct time and place, and for the right reasons. Reciprocally, the unmistakable sign of a lady or gentleman is the rendering of appropriate honors.

Gentleness

Gentleness pertains to anger. The extremes are irritability and slowness to anger. Like so many of Aristotle's virtues, the idea is to express anger **correctly**. Think of the expression intended to remind the journalist about the necessary contents of her article: "who, what, when, where, why, and how." Aristotle expects a virtuous person to be angry (what) at the right person (who), in the right way (how), at the right time and place (when and where), and for the right reason (why).

No formula can be given for determining gentleness. The myriad details of the actual circumstances are determinative. The judgment of any virtue is a perception. A lady or a gentleman knows a virtuous action when she or he sees it. "That was a beautiful thing to do."

A great fictional example of perfectly expressed anger appears in the 2008 Clint Eastwood film *Gran Torino*. Clint Eastwood's character, Walt, is a grumpy old retired widower. He befriends a teenaged neighbor, Thao, who is the victim of gang violence. Walt needs to exact revenge for a particularly brutal assault on Thao's sister, Sue. Thao wants to kill the gang members. Walt, mature and cautious, reflects for days on what he promises will be a massive reprisal. Walt decides to trick the gang into killing the unarmed Walt. Walt is massacred by the gang members in a hail of bullets in the front yard of the gang's hangout. The entire gang is arrested for murder of Walt, the unarmed and "harmless" old man. Thus, Thao and Sue are avenged and saved.

No tough-guy-Clint-Eastwood character should die in a hospital plugged into machines. A hail of bullets is the only way for a tough-guy-Clint-Eastwood character to die beautifully. As General George S. Patton (1885–1945) says in the 1970 film *Patton*: "There's only one proper way for a professional soldier to die: the last bullet of the last battle of the last war."

One has to see the movie, but Walt's revenge is beautiful and virtuous in every Aristotelian sense. Beauty is a perception.

As Fabian Libertarians soon to be the target of sociopathic Leviathan, we will certainly have opportunities to practice the Aristotelian virtue of gentleness.

Truthfulness

According to Aristotle the extremes of which truthfulness is the mean are exaggeration and understatement. Exaggeration stretches the truth toward bragging. Understatement minimizes the truth toward irony. The type of truth under consideration here does not pertain to contracts and matters of justice and injustice, but rather to claims one might make about oneself. Aristotle advises that most ladies and gentlemen will tend toward the ironic, as in the case of Socrates (470–399 BC), who famously declared the he knew nothing. Socrates' "wisdom" was precisely in the knowledge that he knew nothing.

Perhaps the single greatest fault among Libertarians and Objectivists, the followers of Ayn Rand (1905–1982), is hubris. We tend to think that we know more than others and we tend to vaunt that superiority over others. Modesty is a virtue and is absolutely essential when attempting to persuade others. Fabian Libertarians must think of ourselves as teachers. Teachers have respect for their students, especially when the teacher-student relationship is voluntary. The teacher-student relationship is **not** voluntary in the case of Leviathan Education.

All voluntary relationships are by definition terminable at will. Our "students" will not tolerate our "teaching" in the absence of personal modesty.

Charm

Charm pertains to playfulness in character. The extremes are buffoonery and boorishness.

Perhaps the most charming person of all time is Alcibiades (450–404 BC). Though far from virtuous otherwise, he excelled in charm. Alcibiades was born in the golden age of ancient Athens during the rule of the great Pericles (495–429 BC). Alcibiades was beloved of the people of Athens, until charged with sacrilege. He escaped to Sparta where he seduced the king's wife. He escaped to Persia to assist the Persians against Athens and Sparta during the Persian interventions in the ongoing Peloponnesian War (431–404 BC). He was welcomed back to Athens after fleeing the Persians. Finally, Alcibiades was assassinated at the command of the Spartan King Lysander (–395 BC) in Phrygia (present-day northwestern Turkey). Evidence of a more charming rouge does not appear in history.

There is no greater pleasure than the company of a charming lady or gentleman. Some of us can only aspire to this virtue. Those Fabian Libertarians possessed of charm will be invaluable in drawing people to our cause.

Friendliness

The extremes of which friendliness is a mean are obsequiousness and churlishness. A flatterer is obsequious. A curmudgeon is churlish. In order to be happy in our relationships and successful in our political efforts, we strive to be friendly.

Sense of Shame

While Aristotle lists a sense of shame among the other virtues, he explicitly says that shame is not a virtue. The extremes are the shy person who is ashamed about everything and the shameless person is ashamed of nothing. Shame is the feeling following the commission of a base act, for example, shoplifting. Because ladies and gentlemen would never commit any base acts, a sense of shame is not a virtue.

The sense of shame is present in ladies and gentlemen only as a potentiality.

Adam Smith (1723–1790) famously said, "What can be added to the happiness of a man who is in health, out of debt, and has a clear conscience?" Let us refrain from base acts in order never to have to experience shame.

Sociopathic Leviathan and sociopaths lack a sense of shame.

Righteous Indignation

The extremes of righteous indignation are joy at the misfortune of others—*schadenfreude*—and envy at the good fortune of others. We need express righteous indignation (what) toward the right person (who), at the right time and place (when and where), for the right reason (why), and in the proper manner (how).

Remember the judgment of the beauty of the action is in the perception. There are no rules for proscribing the conduct of ladies and gentlemen.

Justice

Aristotle's justice is complete virtue in relation to someone else. Fabian Libertarians seek, above all, to bring justice to all Americans. Aristotle says, "It must not be forgotten that what is being sought is not only what is ***just*** simply but what is ***just*** in political life. And this is found among those who share a life that aims at being ***self-sufficient*** and among those who are ***free*** and are ***equal***"[48] (emphasis supplied). The word "self-sufficient" is crucial to our problem and to our solution.

In order to fully understand our problem, we must look to the root. America is based upon the values of the Enlightenment. The Enlightenment is based upon the values of ancient Greece. The values of ancient Greece derive from the character of people who lived there.

Victor Davis Hanson makes clear in his book *The Other Greeks: The Family Farm and the Agrarian Roots of Western Civilization* that **the citizens who mattered in the polis period** (the era of Greek city-states from 700 to 300 BC) were the **yeoman farmers**. These men owned and farmed their own land. They dealt face-to-face with the realities of agriculture, viniculture, arboriculture, animal husbandry, weather, rocky land, lack of water, disease, pests, sanitation, difficult neighbors, bandits, war parties, family matters, household economics, and so on. They faced reality with their families and subordinates. They succeeded or they died. Their relationship with reality was immediate and final. The virtues necessary for such a life include courage, resourcefulness, self-reliance, fierce independence, individualism, and productivity. The Greek yeoman was farmer, citizen, and soldier. As a citizen, the Greek farmer personally participated in meetings of the people of Athens at the Pynx, a meeting hillside about three thousand feet from the Acropolis. If the demos voted to go to war, the farmer **himself** went to war and immediately. He fought in a Greek phalanx with his fellow yeoman farmers. Their battles were quick (less than one day), violent, and decisive.

Most of us cannot imagine the life of a yeoman farmer in Attica. America was founded by men such as these. Our founding fathers and mothers were yeoman farmers.

One objection to Victor Davis Hanson's book is that he seems to suggest a kind of historical determinism. The life of the yeoman farmer determined, inexorably, his character: courageous, independent, and productive. That character is reflected in the writings of the poets, playwrights, and philosophers of the time. Let us hope that historical determinism is not true. Let us hope that human beings are capable of **willing** the character of a yeoman farmer and can act from the yeoman's moral center. We Libertarians, at least in theory, aspire to this character.

Unlike ancient Greece, the yeoman farmers are not today "citizens who matter." Who, in our time, are the "citizens who matter"? He is not the yeoman farmer. Less than 2 percent of Americans live on farms.[49] The quintessential "citizen who matters" is the thirty-year-old unemployed unmarried man living in his mother's basement watching television from the couch or playing video games. He is slovenly. He is overweight. He is incapable of punctuality. He does not know how to do anything except load a video game. His character is the opposite of courageous, resourceful, capable, self-reliant, fiercely independent, blunt to a fault, individualistic, and productive. Basement Boy of today is a coward, clueless about how or why to live, dependent, Socialistic, and slothful. He and his mother, who defends him, are the creations of Leviathan. He and his mother will always believe the rationale (the lie) for Leviathan's programs. They must, since they have not a clue what to do without Leviathan. Basement Boy and his mother are our "enemy." They are as morally far from the virtuous Greek farmer and our virtuous founding fathers and mothers as slugs are from the gods.

Conclusion of Act One

Be Ladies and Gentlemen. Be Ladies and Gentlemen even should you choose not to become a Fabian Libertarian. To be a lady or a gentleman is to embody Aristotle's virtues: courage, temperance, generosity, magnificence, magnanimity, appetite for honor, gentleness, truthfulness, charm, friendliness, sense of shame, righteous indignation, and justice. Ladies and Gentlemen are virtuous because that is The Beautiful thing to do. The Beautiful cannot be calculated. Beauty is a perception. "That is a beautiful thing to do!" Being a beautiful person is an end in itself. The culminating virtue, the Aristotelian virtue that contains them all, is justice. Be just in all dealings with your fellows.

Chapter 7—The Plan: Act Two

The assumption of Act One of our plan to restore American Freedom, *Look to Our Own Moral Characters*, is that a free society depends upon the presence of ladies and gentlemen in significant numbers among the citizen body. Act One of our Plan is loosely drawn from the decision of Quintus Fabius Maximus Cunctator (280–203 BC) to require the Romans to attend to religious matters after their great loss at the Battle of Trasimene (June 24, 217 BC). Act Two is likewise drawn from the actions of Fabius Maximus in response to the Carthaginian general Hannibal (247–183 BC).

Fabius Maximus, as a Roman general, was well aware of the weather and terrain of Italy. Fabian Libertarians, too, must be well aware of our potential fields of political battle. In the sections that follow, weather is a metaphor for learning the rules of politics and terrain is a metaphor for the political offices to seek.

Learn the Rules

Obey the law. Obey the law. Obey the law. Leviathan has created many laws to protect itself. Leviathan's main defense is to catch naïve idealists who inadvertently violate Leviathan's rules. Even if no conviction results from an alleged violation of the myriad laws, or the punishment following conviction is trivial, the psychological effect on the naïve idealist will be to remove him permanently as a political player. Sociopaths are much better at politics because of their relative emotional insensitivity. In order to avoid Leviathan's prime defense (legal prosecution of its enemies), Fabian Libertarians must be completely familiar with the applicable statutes, and they must strictly follow them all.

The laws of every jurisdiction in which a Fabian Libertarian acts must be read, studied, taught, and obeyed. County ordinances, municipal ordinances, state laws and regulations, and federal laws and regulations must be cataloged and learned. Fortunately, these regulations, laws, and ordinances are available online.

Local Sign Ordinance

A common local ordinance pertains to signs. The ubiquitous campaign yard sign is an oft used method of political communication. The local signage ordinance must be carefully read and followed. Here is one example from Section 8.3 of the Clayton County, Georgia, Code of Ordinances:

1) The property owner must give permission for all sign placement on the owner's property. Signs are not permitted in the State right-of-way, and shall only be located in the County right-of-way with proper approval from the Clayton County Department of Transportation and Development.
2) All signs and sign structures, except as noted below must be setback at least ten (10) feet from the public right-of-way. No portion of a sign or sign structure erected on private property shall encroach on or overhang the public right-of-way without proper approval from the Clayton County Department of Transportation and Development, or be located upon any other person's property.

Campaign workers commonly place signs in the public right-of-way and upon private property without permission, usually because they lack proper training. The most benign government response to illegal sign placement is the removal of the signs by county workers without further action. Expensive campaign signs are thus lost to the landfill. There is no reason, though, why a police detective could not contact the candidate to ask why he has placed his campaign signs illegally. The intimidation factor of such police contact should not be underestimated. Furthermore, there is no reason why a prosecutor could not charge the candidate or his campaign workers with crimes. Politics is not for babies. Compliance with a sign ordinance may seem trivial, but incumbent politicians and their incumbent friends in the sheriff's office and in the prosecutor's office can be expected to use every legal method to take out the competition.

Candidate Qualifications

State law will be the primary source of election law, especially in local and state elections. State constitutions define the qualifications for office. Here is one example from the Georgia Constitution, Article III, Section II, Paragraph III, Qualifications of member of General Assembly:

a) At the time of their election, the members of the Senate shall be citizens of the United States, shall be at least 25 years of age, shall have been citizens of this state for at least two years, and shall have been legal residents of the territory embraced within the district from which elected for at least one year.
b) At the time of their election, the members of the House of Representatives shall be citizens of the United States, shall be at least 21 years of age, shall have been citizens of this state for at least two years, and shall have been legal residents of the territory embraced within the district from which elected for at least one year.

The age limitation is important because part of our one-hundred-years plan to restore American Freedom will be to focus on very young candidates in order to prepare them for long careers in politics as Fabian Libertarians. The ideal first political office is state representative. Your daughter, a 21-year-old Fabian Libertarian, elected to the state house in 2020 might become President of the United States in 2100! (Life spans will become longer and longer as we execute our one-hundred-years plan.)

Lobbyist Defined

Another trap that comes close to violating our constitutional right to free speech is the regulation of lobbyists. An Atlanta-based radio talk show host was heard to complain that Leviathan Big Government had threatened him with prosecution for "lobbying" without a license because the host was haranguing a legislator on his radio talk show. Let us read *a part of a subsection* in the definitions portion of the Georgia lobbyists' statute. See if we can even begin to understand what a "lobbyist" is under Georgia law OCGA § 21-5-70 (5). Most states will have laws like this.

"Lobbyist" means:

(A) Any natural person who, either individually or as an employee of another person, receives or anticipates receiving more than $250.00 per calendar year in compensation or reimbursement or payment of expenses specifically for undertaking to promote or oppose the passage of any legislation by the General Assembly, or any committee of either chamber or a joint committee thereof, or the approval or veto of legislation by the Governor;

(B) Any natural person who makes a lobbying expenditure of more than $1,000.00 in a calendar year, not including the person's own travel, food, lodging expenses, or informational material, to promote or oppose the passage of any legislation by the General Assembly, or any committee of either chamber or a joint committee thereof, or the approval or veto of legislation by the Governor;

(C) Reserved;

(D) Any natural person who, either individually or as an employee of another person, is compensated specifically for undertaking to promote or oppose the passage of any ordinance or resolution by a public officer specified under subparagraph (F) or (G) of paragraph (22) of Code Section 21-5-3, or any committee of such public officers, or the approval or veto of any such ordinance or resolution;

(E) Any natural person who makes a lobbying expenditure of more than $1,000.00 in a calendar year, not including the person's own travel, food, lodging expenses, or informational material, to promote or oppose the passage of any ordinance or resolution by a public officer specified under subparagraph (F) or (G) of paragraph (22) of Code Section 21-5-3, or any committee of such public officers, or the approval or veto of any such ordinance or resolution;

(F) Any natural person who as an employee of the executive branch or judicial branch of local government engages in any activity covered under subparagraph (D) of this paragraph;

(G) Any natural person who, for compensation, either individually or as an employee of another person, is hired specifically to undertake influencing a public officer or state agency in the selection of a vendor to supply any goods or services to any state agency but does not include any employee or independent contractor of the vendor solely on the basis that such employee or independent contractor participates in soliciting a bid or in preparing a written bid, written proposal, or other document relating to a potential sale to a state agency and shall not include a bona fide salesperson who sells to or contracts with a state agency for goods or services and who does not otherwise engage in activities described in subparagraphs (A) through (F) or (H) through (I) of this paragraph;

(H) Any natural person who, either individually or as an employee of another person, is compensated specifically for undertaking to promote or oppose the passage of any rule or regulation of any state agency;

(I) Any natural person who, either individually or as an employee of another person, is compensated specifically for undertaking to promote or oppose any matter before the State Transportation Board; or

(J) Any natural person who makes a lobbying expenditure of more than $1,000.00 in a calendar year, not including the person's own travel, food, lodging expenses, or informational material, to promote or oppose any matter before the State Transportation Board.

The point of setting out this statutory definition is to illustrate the labyrinthine rules that exist. We notice that the definition references to other statues that we must examine to learn what is forbidden. The law is vague enough to allow a disgruntled incumbent legislator to threaten the free speech rights of a talk show host. These are snares for the unwary and are intended to keep outsiders, including Fabian Libertarians, out.

Use of State Seal

Here is another good one. This law forbids the use of the seal of the State of Georgia to nonincumbent. OCGA § 50-3-32:

(a) As used in this Code section, the term "election" means any primary election; run-off election, either primary or general; special election; general election; or recall election.
(b) Every constitutional officer; every official elected state wide; the executive head of every state department or agency, whether elected or appointed; each member of the General Assembly; and the executive director of each state authority shall be authorized to use or display the great seal or a facsimile of the state emblem for official state purposes and, in addition, each of the officials enumerated in this subsection who are elected officials shall be authorized to use or display the great seal or a facsimile of the state emblem on or in connection with any campaign poster, sign, or advertisement for election to any public office.
(c) Except as otherwise authorized by Code Section 50-3-31 or subsection (b) of this Code section, it shall be unlawful for any person, firm, corporation, or campaign committee to use or display the great seal or a facsimile of the state emblem on or in connection with any campaign poster, sign, or advertisement for election to any public office in such a manner as to falsely suggest or imply that the person on whose behalf the same is used is at the time a holder of a public office for which a commission bearing said seal is used.
(d) Any person who violates any provision of subsection (c) of this Code section shall be guilty of a misdemeanor.

The discovery of this rule by most candidates would be accidentally before committing the crime or upon the occasion of a police detective's questioning after the crime is committed. Every state will have a number of different traps for the unwary.

Many More Laws

Each state will have extensive laws and regulations governing the registration of candidates and candidates' committees. For example, Georgia Election Code, Title 21, Chapter 2. There are complex reporting requirements for contributions and expenditures. For example, Georgia Election Code, Title 21, Chapter 5.

The laws set out above are simply a few local examples of the labyrinth of laws and regulations that every Fabian Libertarian is required to navigate.

Army generals must concern themselves with weather and terrain, among other factors of war. The laws and regulations governing the particular jurisdiction are analogous to the weather. The political offices to seek are analogous to the terrain of battle. Let us look at political offices next.

Political Offices

There are many elected offices at the local, state, and federal levels. Familiarity with these offices is part of learning our terrain for political battle. As we are very early in our fight, Fabian Libertarians must think of ourselves primarily as *educators* of our children, our families, our communities, fellow politicians, and the public at large. We should not anticipate actually changing laws in the direction of freedom anytime soon. Educators benefit from positions of authority. Elected office is a position of authority. Our immediate goal should be to get Fabian Libertarians elected to office in order that they be more effective educators, as well as great role models. The argument of this section is that Fabian Libertarians should target state legislatures first.

Not Fabian Target Offices

Generally speaking, Fabian Libertarians do not run for office because they need a job. Fabian Libertarians run for office because they want to restore American Freedom. Some elected positions are simply jobs that need to be performed and performed well. These jobs include police chiefs, sheriffs, magistrate judges, probate judges, state court judges, superior court judges, state-level appellate court judges, water authorities, and boards of education. While incidentally having Libertarians in these posts may insure that Fabian Libertarians are not unfairly targeted by Leviathan, at least locally, the offices are not a world-changing Fabian Libertarian priority. Any Libertarian in any government office is likely to perform her task better because of her Libertarian philosophy. Better government is likely to result with a Libertarian in office.

The Sheriff's Office

Sheriff's deputies serve arrest warrants, serve civil process papers, staff local jails, protect the court system, and engage in general law enforcement, including the enforcement of traffic laws. To be the sheriff—the boss of sheriff's deputies—is an important and good job. The sheriff has no option other than to follow the laws as they are written and swears an oath to do so. The sheriff's position is not legislative. It is unseemly for a sheriff, as a sheriff, to advocate major legislative changes.

What is said of the sheriff's office is true of any appointed or elected law enforcement position, whatever it is called in a particular jurisdiction.

A law enforcement office is not an appropriate ground for the Fabian Libertarian fight for American Freedom.

The Probate Court

Probate courts issue marriage licenses, death certificates, residency certificates, and weapons carry permits. Probate courts supervise the administration of decedent estates and guardianships and conservatorships. To be the probate judge is an important and good job. The probate judge has no option other than to follow the laws as they are written and swears an oath to do so. The probate judge's position is not legislative. It is unseemly and against the judicial canons of ethics for a judge to advocate legislation or to express political opinions.

What is said of the probate court is true of all courts on any level, whatever they are called in a particular jurisdiction.

Judgeships are not an appropriate ground for the Fabian Libertarian fight for American Freedom.

The Water Authority

The water authority runs the municipal water supply. Water and sewer service is a business ***inappropriately*** operated by a government agency. Libertarians advocate the privatization of most government services, including the delivery of water and sewer services. Until water and sewer services are privatized toward the end of our one-hundred-years fight for American Freedom, public utilities will have to continue to function well. Water authorities are not legislative.

What is said of the water authority is true of all public utilities, whatever they are called in a particular jurisdiction.

Elected or appointed officials for public utilities are not an appropriate ground for the Fabian Libertarian fight for American Freedom.

The Board of Education

A board of education operates the government schools in a particular jurisdiction. Education is a business ***inappropriately*** operated by a government agency. Libertarians advocate the complete privatization of education. Until education is privatized toward the end of our one-hundred-years fight for American Freedom, public education will have to continue to function well. Boards of education sometimes have taxing authority for school revenue, but are not otherwise legislative.

Boards of education are not an appropriate ground for the Fabian Libertarian fight for American Freedom.

On the other hand, as customer of Government Education, a parent or interested citizen might well chose to serve on a board of education. Her goal, though, is to insure a better education for her children. Eliminating public education from within a board of education is not possible, though special insight, from a position on the board of education into the evil public education does, would be useful in the Fabian Libertarian effort to privatize education.

United States Congress

While Fabian Libertarians hope for Libertarians in Congress, *success* running for Congress will have to wait until substantial progress is made in the state legislatures. Former Texas Congressman Ron Paul (1935–) is a Libertarian who served in the United States House of Representatives from 1997 until 2013, but **he ran for Congress as a Republican**. Congressman Paul mostly voted "no" while in Congress, as he should have.

While Libertarians will continue to run for Congress and for President of the United States every year from now until forever, those high offices are *not* an immediate part of the Fabian Libertarian Plan.

Fabian Target Offices

The following offices are good terrain for our one-hundred-years fight for American Freedom.

The Board of County Commissioners

The board of commissioners operates the county in which it is located. The board of commissioners has authority for the hiring and firing of county employees, creates an annual budget, imposes taxes, authorizes expenditures, and enacts county ordinances.

A Libertarian on the local governing board can influence legislation. Opposing higher taxes and wasteful spending will always be an important task for Fabian Libertarians. Also, inappropriate regulation of business can be opposed as an elected official on the local government body. The 2015 push to regulate personal trainers (!) in the District of Columbia could use a few Libertarian opponents on the D.C. city council.

Running for local offices is easier than running for state or national offices. The number of voters required to persuade is smaller in local elections. The money spent by local candidates is less than state and national candidates. The time necessary to win a local election is less than that required when running for state and national offices. The number of necessary campaign workers is less.

Perhaps the greatest good from running for and winning positions on the board of commissioners or city councils will come from the experience of running and governing. A Fabian Libertarian county commissioner will have an authoritative position from which to educate others.

State Legislature

The state legislature is the ideal battleground for the restoration of American Freedom.

First, the threshold age for candidacy is very young. As indicated earlier, in Georgia the minimum age to be elected to the House of Representatives is twenty-one. The minimum age to be elected to the Senate is twenty-five. The Fabian Libertarian plan is to focus our efforts on young candidates. Young people are more appealing to the electorate. The training of young Fabian Libertarians will pay dividends in the future.

Second, a legislator can say "no" more easily than an executive. Government must continue to work while Fabian Libertarians fight for American Freedom. The electorate must be educated for freedom. (Remember most people in the 1999 fantasy film *The Matrix* are not ready to "take the red pill." The people chained in the cave of Plato's *Republic* are not ready to see the light of Truth.) The electorate will not tolerate an executive who just says "no" and interferes with the smooth functioning of government. A state executive is charged with executing the existing laws of the state, even the bad laws (and most are bad). Most laws are not Libertarian laws. Any law outside the legitimate functions of government—the police, the courts, and national defense—is not a Libertarian law. By far the great bulk of laws in existence and the great bulk of laws passed every legislative session are not Libertarian laws. State legislative offices are preferable to state executive offices because the executives are **required** to execute the laws that the legislature passes, even if the executive happens to be a Libertarian.

A Fabian Libertarian state legislator will spend most of her time saying "no." In a Fabian Libertarian free world, a state legislature would have very little to do. A legislature need outlaw murder, kidnapping, rape, armed robbery, burglary theft, fraud, and assault and battery only once. The state criminal code needs no new laws. We could do with a lot fewer crimes. The only other activity of a state legislature is to create a budget to run the state until the next legislative session. Since the only legitimate government functions are the police, the courts, and national defense, state funding need only be for the state police and the courts. National defense is the task of the Federal Government.

Ideally, legislators would be *volunteers* and would receive **no salary**. They would need to show up for only a few days in order to debate and vote on the state budget. **One vote and done.** Go home! Please! A Fabian Libertarian will garner headlines every year when she reintroduces her bill to eliminate salaries for state representatives and state senators.

On the fringe of political theory, Fabian Libertarians, once in the majority, might consider modifying the method of selection of state representatives and senators. Selection by lot from among qualified citizen volunteers for the offices is not without historical precedent. Ancient Athens, the birthplace of democracy, chose some officers by lot. In addition, subjecting departing legislators to lawsuits by disgruntled citizens on the charge of voting for **unconstitutional legislation** would encourage cautious voting by volunteer legislators. One can only dream.

Conclusion of Act Two

Act Two of our plan is:

1) Fabian Libertarians must learn and obey the labyrinthine election laws.
2) Fabian Libertarians will target local legislative bodies like county boards of commissioners and city councils. The value of running for these offices is as training grounds for running and governing. Also, a commissioner or a council woman will have an authoritative platform from which to educate others.

3) Fabian Libertarians will mostly target state legislative offices. Saying "no" from these offices will not disrupt the functioning of government. Government must continue to operate according to the law until the law is changed. A state representative or a state legislature will speak authoritatively on widespread government corruption. She will be able to point out pork barrel projects costing taxpayers millions of dollars. She will be able to educate others from her high position.

Federal offices will have to wait for the full attention of **Fabian** Libertarians until we have achieved victories on the state level. Fabian Libertarians fully expect that other Libertarians will continue to seek federal offices. From the standpoint of the **Fabian** Libertarian plan to restore American Freedom, such actions can be seen as diversionary tactics.

Fabius Maximus expected Rome to defeat Carthaginian general Hannibal *someday*. Fabius did not predict when the final victory would occur. In fact, the Second Punic War (218–201 BC) did not end until after the death of Fabius Maximus in 203 BC. Hannibal did not die until 183 BC, twenty years after the death of Fabius.

Chapter 8—The Plan: Act Three

Avoid the Enemy

Looking again to Quintus Fabius Maximus Cunctator for guidance, we note again that the epithet *Cunctator* means delayer. Fabius became famous for his strategy of avoiding direct confrontations with the Carthaginian general Hannibal. Fabius would camp his army in mountainous country in the vicinity of the Carthaginians. Fabius was near enough to be threatening to Hannibal, but far enough away to withdraw in the event of an attempted Carthaginian attack. Fabius hoped to wear out Hannibal over the long haul. And a long haul it was. Hannibal would remain in Italy for the next fifteen years, finally being recalled to Carthage in 203 BC. The Second Punic War would not end until 201 BC. The Father of Roman Poetry, Ennius (239–169 BC), says of Fabius, "*Unus homo nobis cunctando restituit rem*" ("One man by delaying restored the state"). Aeneas on his trip to the underworld near the end of Book VI of *The Aeneid* by Virgil (70–19 BC) meets and praises Fabius Maximus using similar words to those of Ennius. Cunctator, originally intended as an insult, became an honorific.

Someone has called Fabius the Father of Guerilla Warfare. Fabius would attack Carthaginian supply lines, stragglers, rear guards, and small patrols. In one famous incident, Fabius tracked Hannibal to Casilinum (near modern-day Naples) where a Carthaginian guide had by error led Hannibal. When Hannibal learned of the guide's error, the guide was crucified. The area, well south of Rome on the Appian Way bounded on the west by Tyrrhenian Sea, is surrounded by mountains. Fabius was able to occupy mountainous positions to the rear of Hannibal's army, apparently trapping the Carthaginians in the valley of Casilinum between the mountains and the sea. Fabius attacked and killed about eight hundred of Hannibal's rear guard.

In a brilliant nighttime move, Hannibal's army was able to escape the Fabian trap. Hannibal's men attached twigs and branches to the horns of two thousand oxen and set them afire. The Carthaginians drove these poor burning beasts through the mountain passes, utterly confusing and terrifying the Romans, who fled their mountain posts, allowing the Carthaginians to escape.

Soft Targets

Libertarians have not had many successes winning state legislative seats. State legislative seats, according to the Fabian Libertarian Plan, are our primary targets. Following Fabius' example, Fabian Libertarians ought to avoid taking the enemy head-on. What this means in state politics is, for example, that we ought not, just yet, run against the speaker of the House of Representatives or the president of the Senate! Fabian Libertarians need *soft targets*.

The Incumbent

One type of soft target is a new legislator who has not yet proved himself to be of great value to Leviathan. An attempt to defeat the "new guy" will not draw the same attention that running against a proven pork-barreler will draw.

Another type of soft target is a legislator who is out of favor with Leviathan. Sometimes legislators refuse to obey Leviathan's orders on grounds of principle or otherwise. Such a legislator might be abandoned by Leviathan.

Another type of soft target is a legislator who has gotten in trouble with the law or has experienced some public scandal. Political opposition to such a legislator will be ignored by Leviathan. Like the Carthaginian stragglers, "Who cares about them?"

The District

Not only must the circumstances of the targeted legislator be considered in determining a soft target, so should the district in which he is found. A "good-ole boy" district is not a soft target. Some districts have intricate networks of businessmen and politicians who have connived together for decades for their mutual political and economic benefit. These enclaves should be avoided in the early years of our one-hundred-years fight to restore American Freedom.

Districts with large populations ought to be avoided. Ballot access is an issue for the Libertarian Party and collecting signatures for petitions where the registered voter population is large is more difficult that in districts with smaller populations.

Districts with a relatively large proportion (when compared with other districts) of young people are to be preferred because young people are freedom-minded. Old Socialists cannot be turned. Therefore, districts with community colleges, colleges, and universities are ideal.

The Fabian Libertarian Candidate

The ideal candidate will be a young person from the district. If she is a former star athlete in high school, valedictorian, yearbook editor, or high school president, so much the better. A good, famous young local resident is the ideal Fabian Libertarian candidate.

Special Statewide Support

Our candidate will receive extraordinary support from Libertarian Party campaign volunteers from all over the state. Hundreds of volunteers will help collect signatures on ballot-access petitions. One hundred volunteers can collect the signatures of twenty thousand registered voters at the rate of two hundred signatures per worker.

The state Libertarian Party will organize volunteers to work social media, to erect yard signs, to prepare mailings, and to make telephone calls for our local Fabian Libertarian candidate.

The state Libertarian Party will provide speakers to promote our candidate across her district. All statewide Libertarian candidates will spend many days in the target district supporting our special Fabian Libertarian candidate. Remember at this stage the likelihood of winning the statewide offices is slim to none. So the statewide Libertarian Party candidates will not be wasting their time by appearing in our targeted state house of representative district to support our Fabian Libertarian candidate. Just imagine the impact of the appearance of the entire statewide Libertarian Party slate of candidates in support of our local Fabian Libertarian candidate.

Let us keep our eye on the ball, to wit: **we want to elect a Fabian Libertarian candidate to the state House of Representatives**. This step is our first and highest priority.

The Aftermath

Win or lose, Fabian Libertarians will learn from our experience. We will refine our techniques. In the event of a loss, we will start over from scratch next election cycle in perhaps an entirely new target district with an entirely new candidate.

If we win, our new Fabian Libertarian Representative will continue to have total state Libertarian Party support. A volunteer aide will accompany our winner to all official events, including, to the extent allowed by law, sessions of the state House of Representatives. A meticulous daily diary of the experiences of our new Fabian Libertarian Representative will be maintained. She will blog her experiences in the state House of Representatives, especially documenting proposed pork barrel legislation. Any legislation beyond funding for the police and the courts is pork, at the state level, except, of course, legislation **repealing** salaries for representatives and senators and repealing any one of hundreds of unnecessary and immoral laws.

Targeting Thugs

The Thugs were a fraternity of professional robbers existing in India from before AD 1356 until after AD 1830. Their modus operandi was to join a traveling caravan pretending to be well-intentioned fellow travelers. The Thugs gained the confidence of the caravanists, traveling hundreds of miles with them if necessary. Members of the Thug gang might join the caravan at different points along the way, slowly gaining a numerical advantage over the hapless travelers. At a strategic moment and place, the Thugs by threes would fall upon a single traveler, holding him on the ground facedown, one Thug restraining the victim's hands, a second restraining the victim's feet, and the third astride the victim's back garroting him with a scarf or a noose. After the travelers are all dead, the goods of the caravan are taken and the dead bodies disposed. The Thugs were a veritable criminal tribe of murderers. Estimates of those killed by Thugs during their six hundred years of existence are as high as one million.

Like the medieval Thugs, our modern mainstream legislators want nothing more than the property of others at any price, usually short of murder. Remember Aristotle's politics:

Aristotle's Politics

	Rule by the one	*Rule by the few*	*Rule by the many*
Good regime	Monarchy	Aristocracy	Polity
Bad regime	Tyranny	Oligarchy	Democracy

Good regimes are characterized by the good intentions of the ruler: the good ruler is interested in the good of the community. Bad regimes are characterized by the bad intentions of the ruler: the bad ruler is interested in the good of the ruler.

These days we endure **Democracy Theater**, meaning that there is only the pretense of democracy. We are actually ruled by an oligarchy, the rule by a few. The oligarchs are wealthy interests groups who buy modern mainstream legislators with their financial support.

Our modern mainstream legislators simply want to expropriate the property of others on behalf of Leviathan. They are not interested in the good of the community (except as a cover story, a rationale). A few of our legislators might even be like the medieval Indian "thugs." They might be ruthless sociopaths who will do anything legal, barely legal, or not all legal to stay in power and achieve the ends of Leviathan. The percentage of legislators who are "thugs" is not obvious and varies from legislative session to session. **What is clear is that our Fabian Libertarian Representative will hear from the thugs**. Perhaps our Fabian Libertarian Representative ought to wear a name tag that says, "Please do not threaten me."

Private threats are common in politics. For example: "You will vote for the governor's budget or you will pay a high price." The nature of the "high price" is not usually made clear, but the threat *is* clear. Our Fabian Libertarian Representative and her aides **will receive threats**, but then they will **take names**.

Our Fabian Libertarian Representative can expect to be taken aside by the minions of powerful legislative leaders and threatened, "**Cooperate or else!**" When this happens, our Fabian Libertarian representative will report this fact to the party and the state Libertarian Party will respond immediately.

The state Libertarian Party will politically **target the thug**. Within one week of the threat, a Fabian Libertarian candidate will file a Notice of Candidacy with the appropriate government office. She will publicly announce her candidacy stating her reason. "I announce my candidacy for the state House of Representatives against incumbent Representative Mr. Thug, because he terrorized my colleague Libertarian Representative Mrs. GoodLady, saying sinisterly, 'Cooperate *or else!*'" A recording of the threat or multiple witnesses to the threat will be necessary.

This strategy will not have as high a priority as our "Soft Targets" strategy because the minions who threaten our Fabian Libertarian Representative will likely be protected by Leviathan. Also, it will not work unless we have a number of Fabian Libertarian candidates-in-waiting in all districts across the state. We will have more and more Fabian Libertarian candidates-in-waiting as we proceed with our one-hundred-years plan to restore American Freedom. Every Fabian Libertarian elected to the state legislature will draw thousands of interested freedom fighters.

Education

A great way to avoid the enemy is to spend time educating the public. Leviathan is largely oblivious to education that occurs outside Government Education. Leviathan will not push back against Fabian

Libertarians who educate the population. Fabian Libertarians will participate in speakers' bureaus to get the word out to local Libertarian Party chapters. Fabian Libertarian candidates in campaign speeches can educate the public about important philosophical and economic matters.

Education also occurs on social media these days. Fabian Libertarians will have to become experts in the use of new media.

There are many subjects about which the public is ignorant *because* they have been educated by Leviathan in Government Schools. A favorite economic confusion is the Luddite Fallacy. Here is an example of the type of lesson Fabian Libertarians will teach.

The Luddite Fallacy

The Luddites were nineteenth-century skilled textile workers who feared "technological unemployment." Headlines alluding to "technological unemployment" are common today. The Luddite Movement took place in Northeastern England between 1811 and 1816. The Luddites' favorite tactic was to destroy newfangled machines that produced hosiery and employed relatively cheaper and unskilled labor to operate the machines. Government spies and troops eventually suppressed the Luddites.

Henry Hazlitt in his famous tome, *Economics in One Lesson* (Harper & Row Publishers, 1946), refutes this oh-so-common fallacy in his chapter VII, "The Curse of Machines." The following refutation draws heavily upon Hazlitt's analysis.

Everybody wants to improve their economic circumstances. We do so by reducing costs and by buying labor saving machines. Seven billion people engage in this process every day. Househusbands clip coupons. Housewives check for the lowest gasoline prices before filling up. Everybody buys a washer, a dryer, and a dishwashing machine to save personal labor performing those tasks. Economizing, using labor saving devices, it is what we do as humans.

In decades past tens of thousands of secretaries typed on IBM Selectric typewriters. Then Savin word processors came into existence and streamed from a cassette tape to a Selectric typewriter a sequence of characters stopping at strategic places to allow the operator to enter the variable word. Then, for $10,000, a businesswoman could buy a word processing machine from Tandy Radio Shack, now bankrupt. Today, the job of secretary is obsolete. Businessmen and businesswomen directly compose in Microsoft Word or Word Perfect whatever it is they need to compose on equipment costing less than $1,000. Nobody uses a typewriter anymore. A Savin word processor is impossible to find and pointless to use. Computers and word processing programs are improved and upgraded regularly.

The key to useful economic analysis is to look for all of the consequences of an economic event. Sure, the enormous market for IBM Selectric typewriters collapsed as a consequence of the personal computer and word processing software. Good economic analysis requires that we look for all the effects of new machines and new labor saving strategies.

As we look for the economic consequences of the introduction of new and improved machines, keep in mind that Leviathan legislates with ***the precise goal of inhibiting the seven billion people on earth from attempting to improve their economic circumstances***. Why else is Uber, the ride sharing company, harassed and inhibited by Leviathan? Uber is a better deal for the consumer and she would, if permitted by Leviathan, use Uber rather than the more expensive and less convenient monopoly taxicab services. Why else is Airbnb.com, the house sharing website, harassed and inhibited by Leviathan? Airbnb.com is a better deal for the consumer and she would, if permitted by Leviathan, use Airbnb.com rather than the more expensive and less convenient Leviathan protected hotels.

Leviathan does not want its subjects to understand economics. Leviathan loves the Luddite Fallacy.

So, what are the other economic consequences of new technology? The consequences include these:

- The new technology must be manufactured, delivered, and maintained (more employment).
- The businesswoman reduces her costs (why else would she employ the new technology) and increases her profits.
    - The new profits can be used to expand her business (more employment).

- The new profits can be used to make outside investments (more employment).
- The profits can be used by the businesswoman for personal consumption (more employment).

• The increased profits of the business will draw new capital to the industry.

- More capital results in increased sales of the new technology (more employment).
- More capital to the industry creates new businesses selling the target product (more employment).

• As a result of increased competition, the price of the product goes down benefiting consumers.

- With the savings from the reduced price, consumers can buy more of the product in question (more employment).
- With the savings from the reduced price, consumers can increase their own personal consumption of other goods (more employment).

A current profession that is going the way of the Luddites is medical radiology. Decades ago a radiology was the best paid medical specialty. Today, with the advent of the Internet, x-rays can be read in any country in the world by any medical doctor in the world. Competition for radiology jobs is intense. As a result, the salaries of radiologists are being cut in half and more. As indicated earlier, medical doctors will be hard-pressed to maintain their high-income status as the Internet takes over their functions.

Ironically, a consequence of new technology is **voluntary** unemployment. No longer do young children **have to work** in order to survive. No longer do Americans **have to work** from sunup to sundown, seven days a week with no vacation. Most American work about forty hours per week and have many holidays, sick days, and paid vacations. This very happy "lack of work" is a beneficent consequence of technology. The population of the world at this writing is over seven billion people. This huge population is possible only ***because*** of technology.

Of course, any able-bodied adult can work 112 hours per week (sixteen hours per day, seven days per week) if he really wants to. Who wants to?

Socialists whine about a minimum wage ***and*** new technology. Technology is the root of human productivity. An individual's productivity determines her economic worth. A person who digs a ditch with a shovel is worth less than the skilled operator of a backhoe. The shovel digger gets the minimum wage, if he is employed at all. The backhoe operator earns much more than the minimum wage. Do not forget that the shovel was once a new technology. Imagine our prehistoric ancestor demanding that his tribal chief forbid the introduction of the shovel because his hand digging job would be made obsolete by the shovel.

Of all the consequences of the introduction of new technology, perhaps the most important is the reduction of the cost of products and services to the consumer. Often it is said that the poorest American today lives a better life that the richest king during the Middle Ages. We have so many products and services today with so little effort. As the goods and services required for the good life go down in price, the amount of labor each of us must exert goes down. These days we work forty hours per week, let us say. We could work even less, but for the grotesque looting of our substance by Leviathan. As we advance into the future, we may fully expect that our workweek will continue to shrink, and we will be able to enjoy more and more blessed free time.

Free time need not be and should not be unproductive time. Even those of us who do not have a regular job, say because we are retired or homemakers, are **very productive without an employer.**

A reason why the Luddite Fallacy persists is a lack of imagination. We cannot imagine what the world would be like without the IBM Selectric, without horse-drawn carriages, or without highly skilled hand weavers replaced by stocking frames, spinning frames, and power looms. We cannot be blamed for failing to imagine the ***specific*** consequences of the introduction of a particular new technology, because seven billion people will be working on that task. A single individual cannot possibly match that brain power. We ***can be blamed*** for failing to learn the lesson of human history, endlessly

FABIAN LIBERTARIANISM

repeated, from prehistoric times to the present: New technology improves our productivity and thus our economic well-being. New and unimaginable economic opportunities will open before us.

Following is a second example of the type of lesson Fabian Libertarians will teach.

Privacy

Concerning their invasion of the privacy of all Americans, the National Security Agency (NSA) actually says on its website: "If you have nothing to hide, you have nothing to fear."[50] The total extent of NSA's surveillance of innocent American's private data is a state secret. Whether NSA has access to the content of every American's telephone calls and for how long or just to the so-called metadata (who is called, when the call is made, how long the call lasts) is unclear. What seems most likely is that **all telephone calls are recorded**, but access to the recording is legally permitted only with a search warrant. NSA on its website says,

> What if we could build a national data warehouse containing information about every person in the United States? Thanks to secret interpretations of the PATRIOT ACT, top-secret Fourth Amendment exceptions allowed by the Foreign Intelligence Surveillance Court, and broad cooperation at the local, state, and federal level, we can!

Yes, indeed. NSA is proud of its capability. Giddy, let us say. Here is NSA's current list of information collected on every American without a warrant:

> In the spirit of openness and transparency, here is a partial list of current and planned future data collection targets:
>
> - internet searches
> - websites visited
> - emails sent and received
> - social media activity (Facebook, Twitter, etc.)

- blogging activity including posts read, written, and commented on
- videos watched and/or uploaded online
- photos viewed and/or uploaded online
- mobile phone GPS-location data
- mobile phone apps downloaded
- phone call records
- text messages sent and received
- Skype video calls
- online purchases and auction transactions
- credit card/ debit card transactions
- financial information
- legal documents
- travel documents
- health records
- cable television shows watched and recorded
- commuter toll records
- electronic bus and subway passes / SmartPasses
- facial recognition data from surveillance cameras
- educational records
- arrest records
- driver license information

That these intrusions can be bragged about and are not a source of widespread public outrage is a clear sign of just how far Americans have fallen from our former love of Freedom.

Imagine if a man walked up to you on the beach and put two fingers under the front of the waistband of your bathing suit and pulled[51] saying: "If you have nothing to hide, you have nothing to fear." Of course, everyone has something to hide! You want to hide from your sadistic boss the fact that you are actively seeking other employment until the time comes to give your two weeks' notice. You want to hide from your children your birth control equipment. You want to hide from the potential buyer of your house your absolute bottom-line price. You want to hide from the prying eyes of your neighbor the completely normal inside operations of your household. You want to hide your properly licensed concealed-carry firearm so as not to cause unnecessary public anxiety.

Privacy is important. We have stuff we want to keep private. We want most of our stuff kept private. Almost none of us are terrorists.

The piece that is missing is that the National Security Agency is not morally different from the pervert trying to look at your genitalia by pulling at waistband of your bathing suit on the beach. NSA is a large group of people. A pervert is one person. What gives one pervert or a large group of people the right to look in your pants? The reference to genitalia might simply be perceived as hyperbole, but the Transportation Security Agency, Leviathan TSA, does actually electronically look at and manually finger genitalia during airport searches.

NSA is, of course, Leviathan Big Government. But that does not make NSA more entitled to look in your pants than the pervert. We are Americans. The government is supposed to be our servant, not our master. Other countries have Sovereigns who have "moral" (in their political theory) and legal superiority over their subjects. That is not the American way.

The philosophical poison pill is Jean-Jacques Rousseau (1712–1778) and his conception of the General Will. As we have discussed, the General Will is the *mystical* will of the people expressed through voting. To be free, according to Rousseau, is to comply with the General Will.

Americans have accepted the idea that Leviathan Big Government is indeed our master, our ruler, our dictator, our parent, our Big Brother, our Sovereign. Anything Leviathan Big Government wants, Leviathan Big Government gets, including the "right" to look in our pants and finger our genitalia.

Leviathan NSA and Leviathan TSA rationalize these grotesque intrusions upon our privacy on the grounds of security. Seemingly many Americans accept this rationale and accept the fingering of their genitalia and the recording of their private telephone conversations.

While our current Democratic Totalitarianism authorizes these intrusions upon our privacy for "safety's sake," like all products and services co-opted by Leviathan, people can provide the products and services, including security, themselves. **We simply lack the imagination**. Seven billion people are at work at all times and places trying to solve problems of productivity. When a government monopoly upon particular product and service is declared, the work of the seven billion people is thwarted.

Leviathan has its rationales (the lie) and its reasons (the truth). The reason for the existence of Leviathan is life and more life, money, and power. The rationale is the answer to any of a thousand questions. Human beings need a thousand things. Leviathan's rationale (the lie) is always to supply one of the thousand things human beings need. Unimaginative Socialists ask:

- In the absence of Leviathan Big Government, who would provide airport security?
- In the absence of Leviathan Big Government, who would provide for our retirement?
- In the absence of Leviathan Big Government, who would provide for our healthcare?
- In the absence of Leviathan Big Government, who would provide for our education?
- In the absence of Leviathan Big Government, who would provide for clean air and water?
- In the absence of Leviathan Big Government, who would provide our roads?
- In the absence of Leviathan Big Government, who would provide for drug safety?
- In the absence of Leviathan Big Government, how would we know what vaccines are necessary?
- In the absence of Leviathan Big Government, would we not all become drug addicts?
- In the absence of Leviathan Big Government, who would provide for fair farm prices?
- In the absence of Leviathan Big Government, would we not all be working for $1 per hour?
- In the absence of Leviathan Big Government, who would provide for food safety?
- In the absence of Leviathan Big Government, who would provide for product safety?
- In the absence of Leviathan Big Government, who would provide for poor people?

- In the absence of Leviathan Big Government, who would protect us from unbridled competition from Uber and Airbnb.com?
- In the absence of Leviathan Big Government, who would protect us from unlicensed personal fitness trainers in Washington, D.C.?
- In the absence of Leviathan Big Government, who would provide me with a college education?

Any human need, even those not yet taken over by Leviathan Big Government, can be placed in this formulaic sentence. The uneducated Socialists of America today lack the imagination necessary to answer any of these questions. Fearing the "unknown" posed by the questions, American Socialists opt for Leviathan Big Government authorized by Jean-Jacques Rousseau's General Will. The General Will is determined by the majority votes of unimaginative Socialists.

Is it not clear that the right to vote is a feeble defense of American Freedom, when voting leads to complete totalitarianism? The United States Constitution and its Bill of Rights is the best defense of American Freedom. Freedom is the societal condition in which private property rights are protected by the rule of law.

While any attempt by one person to imagine solutions to the problems of human survival will fall short of the spectacular reality of the results of the thought of seven billion free people, let us do a little imagining about airport security as an example.

Some people would like greater security on airplanes, some less. Consider some possibilities, if free enterprise were allowed to solve the problems.

- One entrepreneur might create an airline with the name "Sheep Airlines." This company would guarantee that any passenger would be strip-searched before being allowed to board. His baggage would be opened and thoroughly inventoried. An interior body x-ray would detect surgically implanted bombs. Digital rectal and gynecological exams would be performed on each passenger. Sheep Airlines is not likely to be successful.

- One entrepreneur might create an airline with the name "Cowboy Airlines." This company would allow passengers to openly carry firearms with no prescreening of passengers or baggage. Cowboy Airlines is very likely to be successful, especially with Texans.
- One entrepreneur might create an airline with the name "Royal Airlines." This company would be a members-only airline. The passengers would all be prescreened prior to membership and treated like members of a private British Gentlemen's Club, ladies allowed, once admitted to membership. Royal Airlines is likely to be very successful, especially among business travelers.
- One entrepreneur might mimic the present system with the name "Same-ole-thing Airlines." This company would continue to employee minimum wage "blue gloves" to screen passengers with uneven customer service, providing the occasional genital grope in the event of workday boredom. Disabled senior citizens and toddlers not exempted. The Same-ole-thing Airlines survives only because of its government monopoly.

There would be dozens of solutions to airline security in the absence of Leviathan Big Government and Leviathan TSA. We simply lack the imagination to conceive of them all. Undoubtedly, some very clever and customer-friendly solutions would be found. Just set the entrepreneurs free!

What about the National Security Agency (NSA) with which we started? Shut the privacy-invading agency NSA down and transfer the assets and legal functions to the Central Intelligence Agency (CIA) which spies on other countries, not on Americans.

At the end of the Third Punic War (149–146 BC), thirty-seven years after the death of Carthaginian general Hannibal, the Romans totally destroyed Carthage by systematically burning it for seventeen days. They razed the walls and buildings to the ground and the salted the earth (nineteenth-century apocrypha?) so that nothing might there again grow. As the first legal act of our Fabian Libertarian United States Congress and presidency after Inauguration Day, Wednesday, January 20, 2117, let our Fabian Libertarian grandchildren enact laws to remove the blight of sites like NSA's Utah Data Center of the Defense Surveillance Directorate (a great Orwellian name)[52] from the face of the earth.

Conclusion to Act Three

Act Three of the Fabian Libertarian plan to restore American Freedom consists of two parts. The first part is to pick **soft targets** for our young Fabian Libertarian candidates. The second part is to **educate** from positions of authority in government. We need to create set speeches and speak them over and over again to remind the public what American Freedom is all about.

These last three chapters state the Fabian Libertarian Plan to restore American Freedom. In the next chapters, we will explore the outer limits of Libertarian theory. These topics will not be relevant until decades hence after we have mostly restored American Freedom.

Chapter 9—No Federal Taxes

One problem Fabian Libertarians must overcome is **doubt about** how a society in which all relationships are voluntary functions. The biggest problem is the apparent necessity of taxes, which are not voluntary. While Libertarian theory has not completely resolved the problem of involuntary taxation, this chapter provides one possible solution on the federal-government level.

Freedom is the protection of private property, including the rights to life, liberty, and the pursuit of happiness, by the rule of law. Freedom is not the right to vote. The right to vote is a (not very effective) tool intended to preserve freedom. Freedom has not been secured in America by the right to vote. Jimmy Carter said on July 28, 2015: "Now [America is] just an oligarchy with unlimited political bribery being the essence . . ."[53]

In Libertarian theory, freedom and responsibility are related. An able adult person is free precisely because she is responsible for her own life. In order to live, to survive and flourish, *a person must be free*. Stated another way, freedom is a condition of human survival. Stated as a condition of survival: "If a human being is to survive, she must be free." **Human action in freedom is the human method of survival and flourishing.** The social ideal for Libertarians is that all adult human relationships be *voluntary*. If both or all parties are not in accord, there is no personal, social, or economic interaction between or among them. Most people understand the principle of voluntarism in their daily lives. If our would-be friends, colleagues, associates, customers, or trading partners *do not want* to relate or trade with us, then there is no relating or trading.

Unfortunately, with the growth of government, has come the creation of many laws and regulations that *force* people to interact in variety of ways. For most people forced relationships are a way of life. Thousands of regulations govern virtually every human economic transaction, rendering them at least partially involuntary. Just think of the regulations governing employment in America, minimum wages, elaborate benefits systems, restrictions on hours of employment, restrictions on termination, and restrictions on work conditions.

Most non-Libertarian readers of this chapter will be happy about such regulations, because non-Libertarians believe in "the Little People" discussed in a previous chapter. "The Little People" are able adults who non-Libertarian elites think could not function without the intervention of Leviathan Big Government. Perhaps there are able adults who do not mind being thought of as "the Little People" by their non-Libertarian elitist "superiors." Non-Libertarian elites believe that "the Little People" would be working in sweatshops and picking agricultural produce for less than substance wages but for Leviathan Big Government.

The modern American Socialist opinion about the relationship between the rich and the poor is this:

> Vous avez besoin de moi, car je suis riche et vous êtes pauvre; faisons donc un accord entre nous: je permettrai que vous ayez l'honneur de me servir, à condition que vous me donnerez le peu qui vous reste, pour la peine que je prendrai de vous commander!» Discours Sur L'Economie Politique (1755), by Jean-Jacques Rousseau.
>
> You have need of me because I am rich and you are poor. Let's make an agreement: I will grant you the honor of serving me on condition that you give what little you have left, in exchange for the trouble I will take to give you orders. [Translation by the author]

Perhaps this was true when written by Rousseau forty-four years before the French Revolution, but it was not true in America until the Socialists took over.

But we stray too far. This chapter is directed to Libertarians. We are not trying to convert non-Libertarian elitists—a hopeless task in any event. Our topic is taxes. Taxes involve the involuntary taking of the private property of another by Leviathan Big Government. Taxes are a violation of the voluntary relationship principle of Libertarianism.

It may come as a surprise to many readers, even non-Libertarian readers, that direct taxation has not always existed. The ancient Greek polis, for example, did not start out with a system of direct taxation. A yeoman farmer in ancient Greece would not have tolerated a tax on his farm or his income.

How, theoretically, might a Libertarian Government function without taxes?

In America, we have multiple layers of government. We have the Federal Government, state governments, and local governments. The problems of running these various governments without a system of taxation are different at every level.

Libertarians need not be convinced that the only legitimate functions of government are the police, the courts, and national defense. Government is defined as the agency invested with the sole right to initiate the offensive use of force. Individuals retain the right to use defensive force. Governments can "offensively" intervene to arrest people, to make and enforce judgments, and to project military power in defense of America. Individuals cannot arrest people, make and enforce judgments, or project military power within a Libertarian society.

If these are the only legitimate functions of the Federal Government, it is easy to imagine that a federal budget might be 10 percent of a federal budget these days. The current federal budget is about four trillion dollars per year. A tenth of that amount is 400 billion dollars. National defense is currently about 570 billion dollars per year. Administration of justice is currently about fifty-four billion dollars per year. General government is about twenty-three billion dollars per year. The total current budget is 647 billion dollars per year considering only legitimate functions of government: police, courts, and the military.

No one reading this chapter will conceive that the current defense budget is reasonable. America engages in too many proxy wars. The budget for "general government" includes over fifty million dollars spent on presidential vacations over the last six years. Libertarians agree that the war on drugs, a large portion of the "administration of justice" budget item, is completely illegitimate. Few will doubt that Congressional pay and benefits, including congressional staff, are grossly excessive.

Correcting "waste and abuse" is a political bromide. We are not talking about that.

The Presidency

Not only should presidential vacations be completely eliminated as a government expense, the presidency should be a volunteer job. The President should not be paid for her work. She should not receive an extravagant lifetime pension upon retirement from office. She should not be protected day and night by a small army. Government service at the federal level ought to be mostly voluntary. An individual is honored to be chosen to lead her nation, especially the United States of America. An individual who is mature enough and successful enough to warrant being chosen President should not need to be supported by the government during her term in office. If she needs extra spending money, she can get a paper route.

In a Libertarian Government, the job of being president would not be full time. A Libertarian president has two jobs: approving or vetoing legislation passed by the Congress and commanding the armed forces. Congress, as we shall shortly see, should not be in session for more than forty days per year. Given this job description, the president need be in Washington, D.C. only time enough to sign next year's budget.

The spectacle of the president's interjecting herself into every social controversy, competing with Kim Kardashian for entertainment media face time, is disgraceful. A president would better serve her country by hosting tours for school children at the White House.

The Congress

Congresswomen are representatives of their various states. Their salaries, if any, ought to be paid by those states. When a person hires an agent to represent her in a negotiation in a distance city, that person bears the expense of the agent. So it should be for congresswomen.

Furthermore, as indicated above, there is no reason for Congress to be in session for more than forty days per year. The only routine business of Congress is to make an annual budget. Rarely, the Congress might be called upon to declare war. Being a congresswoman or a senator ought to be a part-time job, just as it is in many state legislatures.

The Federal Courts

The Federal Courts are engaged in the war on drugs and in resolving disputes involving federal agencies, most of which will cease to exist in a Libertarian Government. The work load of the Federal Courts is likely to drop to 1 percent of the current load in a Libertarian environment. If the current budget is seven billion dollars, 1 percent of that amount is seventy million dollars.

Operating a court tends to be a full time job for judges and clerks. Contrary to popular suspicion, most lawyers are not independently wealthy and, therefore, cannot support themselves *and* be full time judges *without pay*. Therefore, federal judges may have to be paid by the Federal Government.

The only federal court that must exist according to the Constitution is the Supreme Court. The Constitution provides that judges "shall receive for their services compensation." If the nine Justices of the Supreme Court received salaries of $200,000 per year that would mean an annual budget amount of $1,800,000. The Court will certainly need a Clerk. Thus the salaries of the Supreme Court might conceivably be less than two million dollars per year.

Under present economic conditions, living in Washington, D.C. on $200,000 per year is no easy task. After the elimination of most of the Federal Government by the installation of a Libertarian Government, Washington, D.C. will become a veritable ghost town compared to its present bloated economic status. Washington Metropolitan Statistical Area (MSA) is the ninth largest MSA currently. After Libertarian Government is installed, the Washington MSA will return to its original small town status.

A two-million-dollar Untied States Supreme Court budget could be paid by a forty thousand dollar tax on each of the fifty states.

Federal Police

There is no need for a federal police force. All policing ought to be performed by the several states and local governments.

The Alphabet Soup of Federal Agencies

None of the many federal agencies, VA, FDA, EPA, HUD, DEA, FBI, CDC, FCC, FTC, NLRB, SSA, SEC, FHA, TSA, ATF, DOJ, DHS, DOE, DOA, DOC, DOL, and so on, would continue to exist under a Libertarian Federal Government. Who cares what the initials stand for? Budget equals zero!

The Military

Thus far we have reduced the federal budget to two million dollars per year for the Supreme Court. The biggest budget item of a Libertarian Federal Government must necessarily be the military: army, navy, air force, marines, and coast guard. How would a Libertarian Government pay for its military?

A clue to the solution is the Second Amendment to the Constitution: "A well-regulated militia being necessary to the security of a free state, the right of the people to keep and bear arms shall not be infringed."

Modern Americans have little sense of the meaning of "a well-regulated militia." We must look back to the ancient Greek polis for a better understanding of this concept. In ancient Greece the yeoman farmer (a person who farms her own land) was the basic political unit. The yeoman farmers were also the hoplite soldiers who assembled, when necessary, to defend the polis from invaders. These hoplite soldiers were not paid by the polis. They provided their own weapons and armor. They left their farms, when necessary, and marched to war with their neighbors, volunteer leaders, and elected generals. The yeoman was farmer, citizen, and soldier.

America maintains a standing army. The soldiers are paid and their weapons and training are supplied by the Federal Government.

The greatest problem with our present means of waging war is that we do so with little psychological cost, except to those families whose children are killed or wounded, and, of course, to the service members who are killed and wounded. The soldiers are volunteers. **These days Congress need not decide to go to war.** The last Declaration of War was made on December 8, 1941, a day after the Japanese attack on Pearl Harbor. These days we do not pay for the wars. We borrow money to finance wars, so much money that it will never be paid back.

Under a Libertarian Government we would return to well-armed and well-regulated militias. Military service would be opened to volunteers of all ages who would provide, by themselves or with the help of patrons, for their own support, training, arming, and insurance in case of death or injury. Such a soldier would cost nothing to the Federal Government. The cost of a soldier, according to the Pentagon, is about 1.3 million dollars per year. Of course, this number is ridiculous and includes the cost of the proverbial $600 hammer.

What we Americans fail to appreciate is the fact that America goes to war these days, not because our farms are at stake due to an invading neighbor city-state, but rather because our leaders think for reasons not necessarily related to national security that war is useful. Allegedly blowing up an aspirin factory might help divert press attention from a Presidential sex scandal. If there were truly a need for war, like the attack on Pearl Harbor on December 7, 1941, most red-blooded Americans would rally to the cause and take up arms.

Consider this proposal: In order to go to war, *a vote for war*, whether by the Congress or by the people in the case of a national referendum, *must be accompanied by a pledge to go to war in person as a solider,* or *personally to fund* one soldier in the war for the duration. A Declaration of War would include a budget for the war. The Vietnam War cost America about one trillion dollars and 58,220 fatal casualties. There were 620,000 fatal casualties in the Civil War. There were 407,300 fatal casualties in World War II. A total of sixty million people were killed. No war would be declared in the absence of sufficient pledges to fund the war as budgeted.

The military adventurism of America would come to an abrupt end.

The problem though of aggressive totalitarian regimes would not be solved by well-armed and well-regulated militias. America needs a deterrent against surprise attacks by wicked world powers. America needs a Central Intelligence Agency (CIA). America needs sufficient military capacity to deter aggressive totalitarian regimes.

A recent ***intelligence spending*** estimate was seventy-one billion dollars. The amount is undoubtedly grossly inflated. If the budget were 10 percent of that amount, seven billion dollars is still a lot of money, about $220 per person per year or about 140 million dollars per state per year.

International intelligence is necessary, but military infrastructure is equally important. The cost to operate an aircraft carrier is reported to be seven million dollars per day. The cost of an aircraft carrier is reported to be thirteen billion dollars. America presently has ten aircraft carriers in service. Aircraft carriers are only a small component of the infrastructure of a modern military force.

We suggested above that the current military budget is about 570 billion dollars per year. Undoubtedly, if America were not participating in 5 to 134 proxy wars (varies according to definition), this budget would be much less.

A Libertarian Government might grant that some limited, secret foreign military aggressions (without a Declaration of War) might be necessary. If, for example, a rogue nation were known by the CIA to be making a nuclear bomb to detonate in New York City, a secret Navy Seal operation to eliminate the risk would be entirely appropriate. Intervention in various civil wars across the globe would not be undertaken by a Libertarian Government.

To fund the present annual military budget would cost about $2,000 per person. Assuming the budget is two times too big, that still is $1,000 per person, or about 320 billion dollars per year. The cost per four person family would be $4,000 per year.

So, how does a Libertarian Government pay for a military that costs $4,000 per family per year? ***The Libertarian Government asks the citizens.***

Americans are not stupid. They realize that the world is a dangerous place. A major function of the President and the Congress must be to make a carefully reasoned case to the American people to fund ***voluntarily*** the military budget at the cost of $1,000 per person per year. Currently, the IRS collects about $9,000 per person per year in taxes.

One thousand dollars per year per person is a small price to pay for ***freedom from taxation*** and for safety from foreign aggression.

Conclusion

We have asserted the basic Libertarian position that the only legitimate functions of government are the police, the courts, and national defense. We have suggested that the office of the president of the United States ought to be an honorary, unsalaried post. We have suggested that Congresswomen, if paid at all, ought to be paid by their constituent states. We have suggested that the United States Supreme Court budget could be two million dollars be year and ought to be paid by a tax by the Federal Government upon state governments. We have suggested that the military be manned, in large part, by voluntary well-armed, well-regulated militias. We have suggested that funding for international intelligence and military infrastructure be funded by ***voluntary payments*** from citizens in an amount equal to about one ninth of the current total federal tax burden. We have suggested that going to war be done by votes accompanied by pledges in manpower and funding sufficient to achieve the stated objective in the Declaration of War.

Most, save our Libertarian readers, will claim this chapter is utopian. We agree that getting to a Libertarian Government is a difficult task. This chapter sketches an outline of what such a government might look like at the federal level. Imagining a free America in which all relationships are voluntary may be utopian, but it surely is hopeful and inspiring.

Chapter 10—Leave No Trace Behind

Libertarianism has two great theoretical problems: the tragedy of the commons and taxation (just dealt with in chapter 9). In Libertarian theory, the meaning of "freedom" is the societal condition in which property rights, including the rights to life, liberty, and the pursuit of happiness, are protected by the rule of law. Property rights are the key because the goal of politics is human survival and flourishing. Human survival and flourishing is possible only by human work. All that is created or produced by individual human work is private property. Individuals work to secure their own survival and flourishing and the survival and flourishing of all that is necessary in her judgment to her life, including her family, friends, associates, and communities. All adult relationships in a Libertarian society are voluntary, that is, freely chosen by every adult participant to any interaction.

The tragedy of the commons is difficult for Libertarians because, by definition, "the commons" is an asset to which property rights do not easily and obviously pertain. Taxation is difficult for Libertarians because "taxation" usually involves the involuntary confiscation of individual private property, thus violating the Libertarian rule that all adult relationships be voluntary.

The "commons" usually refers to air and water. Even the boldest totalitarian theorist or grasping world monopoly does not yet claim ownership of the earth's atmosphere or of the oceans, though to be sure they savor the thought. *Total Recall*, the 1990 Arnold Schwarzenegger sci-fi film, shows the administrator of the planet Mars withholding company-owned oxygen from an oppressed population. The plot resolves with the creation of a previously nonexistent Mars-wide atmosphere freely available to all inhabitants.

Communist Countries

In formerly communist countries, the "commons" included more than the oceans or the atmosphere. By definition of "communism," all property is "commons." Private property is forbidden. Large tracts of land and parks can be the "commons." The office refrigerator can be the "commons." The tragedy of the commons is that everyone will use the "commons" and no one will care for it. Thus, the office refrigerator becomes dirty and useless after a short time. A "commons" park will be shortly covered in dog poop and other litter, the lawns overgrown with weeds, the flowers gone wild, every fixed structure defaced, and the benches stolen or destroyed. The "commons" shortly become unusable by humans.

The atmosphere in Beijing, China is smog-filled because people and government-run industries dump pollution into the "commons" of the atmosphere. Environmentalists allege that there is a Great Pacific garbage patch containing mostly plastic debris discharged by human beings from land and sea. Assuming that the Great Pacific garbage patch is real and not merely enviro-propaganda, it is an example of the tragedy of the commons.

People of all political persuasions, Right, Left, and Libertarian, believe in clean air and water. The problem is how to achieve the righteous goal of clean air and water. To be sure, there are many people who do not believe in clean air and water, but they are not categorizable as Right, Left, or Libertarian. These are venal people. Venal people litter because it is easier to toss the beer can on the "commons" (roadway, waterway, public park) than to find a trash can. There are venal industrialists who dump pollutants into streams, rivers, oceans and atmosphere, because it is far cheaper than recycling or otherwise rendering safe their own waste products. There are venal politicians who, knowing full well that an unfunded and unfundable pension program is a long-range impossibility, nevertheless create the program to further their own immediate political ambitions. The bankruptcy of the city (Detroit), the state (Illinois), the country (Greece) will occur on somebody else's watch. Libertarians lament that this form of governmental corruption is ubiquitous. The creation of unfunded pension programs is the tragedy of the commons carried to an extreme, where the "commons" is "other people's money" and everything is ruined.

So what is the Libertarian solution for the tragedy of the commons?

Privatize Public Property

The first step is to privatize as much property as is possible. A privately owned park is preferable to a public park. A privately owned farm is preferable to a public cooperative. A privately owned railroad is preferable to a government operated railroad, like Amtrak. A privately owned package delivery company, like UPS or FedEx, is preferable to a governmental monopoly, like the United States Postal Service.

Even after massive privatizations, the atmosphere, the oceans, seas, enormous lakes, rivers and streams will remain a part of the "commons." Human beings live in the biosphere. The biosphere is the quintessential "commons." How does Libertarian theory propose to preserve the biosphere in order that human beings can survive and flourish?

Freedom and Responsibility

Libertarians believe in freedom *and* responsibility. These two are opposite sides of the same coin. In Libertarian theory, the individual should be free *because* he is responsible for her own life. Human freedom is the means of human survival and flourishing. Individual human life is the standard of moral and political law. Because human life is good, human freedom is good. The purpose of politics is to organize human society to optimize human survival and flourishing. Human survival and flourishing is optimized when individuals are free to exercise their minds and bodies to secure their survival and flourishing by the production of private property.

In Libertarian theory, the individual produces goods and services to trade with others in order to create a flourishing life for herself and her family. The individual uses her property in order to flourish. The individual trades her property with others in order to flourish. The individual does not use the property of another without the other's permission (the voluntary association principle).

So, we combine a number of facts and principles:

1. Human beings live in the biosphere. There are exchanges between human beings and the biosphere, intakes (clean air and clean water) and discharges (human waste, exhaled breath, and home, work and industrial waste).
2. In order for human beings to survive and flourish (the goal of ethics and politics), the intakes and discharges to the biosphere must be managed to maintain a healthy-for-human-beings biosphere.
3. The amount of human intakes and discharges that the biosphere can naturally process is a scientific question. For example, humans breathe in oxygen and exhale carbon dioxide. For example, humans drink clean water and discharge urine and feces. Carbon dioxide, urine, and feces must be processed, somehow, by the environment or by human work in order to maintain a balanced and therefore healthy-for-human-beings biosphere. More problematic than these simple biological human discharges are the discharges from human industry, such as waste paper and gaseous discharges from coal-fired power plants.

Combining these principles we come to our new Libertarian speculation: "Leave No Trace Behind." The "Leave No Trace" principles are widely known in outdoor activities circles. The United States Forest Service promotes these seven "Leave No Trace" principles:

- Plan ahead and prepare.
- Travel and camp on durable surfaces.
- Dispose of waste properly.
- Leave what you find.
- Minimize campfire impacts.
- Respect wildlife.
- Be considerate of other visitors.

Applied to the tragedy of the commons, the principle would be that each individual should discharge only that amount of waste that can be processed by the biosphere and not interfere with the intakes of another individual. So, for example, human breathing is not likely to be a problem, since the biosphere can easily process human exhalant. So, for example, human urinating or defecating at sea from a private sailboat is not likely to be a problem, since the biosphere can easily process one human being's waste in the open ocean. Imagine whale poop!

Problems arise when the millions of inhabitants of New York City propose to discharge their collective human waste (urine and feces) into the Hudson River. Such a policy cannot work and is not the current practice, we hope. Problems arise when a coal-fired power plant discharges untreated smoke upwind from a major metropolitan area. Coal-fired power plants are one of the causes of air pollution in Beijing.

The details of a "Leave No Trace Behind" solution will be complex. The general solution is to allow a private cause of action by all individuals harmed by a polluter for monetary damages and injunctive relief to stop any individual or industry from discharging waste into the biosphere in such a way as to damage the complainant. Courts and perhaps legislatures will have to define, based upon scientific evidence, the amount of discharge that does not cause harm to individuals.

A starting principle is that each individual is entitled to receive from the biosphere clean air. A starting principle is that each individual is entitled to experience clean water in large bodies of water (oceans, large lakes) and water courses (streams and rivers) located in the "commons."

Examples

Some examples may be helpful:

When an individual is enjoying his backyard hammock on his own private property, he is entitled to clean air. Thus, a smoker in the vicinity of the property line may be violating the nonsmoker's rights if the smoker's discharge wafts onto the nonsmoker's property and disturbs the nonsmoker's hammock nap. The nonsmoker has the right to ask the smoker to move away from property line in order that the nonsmoker can enjoy his right to clean air. The smoker retains the right to smoke on his own private property, just so long as his smoking discharge does not interfere with the nonsmoker's right to clean air.

On the other hand, if a nonsmoker is visiting a privately owned motel and the policy of the motel owner is to allow smoking anywhere on the property, then the nonsmoker must accept the unsanitary conditions of the motel as a condition of being permitted on the private property by the motel owner.

When an individual is driving to St. Simon's Island, Georgia, she is entitled to clean air. Thus, the stink of a paper plant may be violating the traveler's rights. The traveler would have a private right of action against the paper plant for violating her rights to clean air.

Some pollutants are odorless and colorless, but nevertheless harmful to human beings, for example, carbon monoxide. A polluter who discharges carbon monoxide in amounts harmful to human beings would likewise be subject to private rights of action by individuals damaged by the discharge.

When an individual is enjoying the ocean, she is entitled to clean water. Thus, a beachgoer, who steps on a used syringe and hypodermic needle hidden in the sand previously discharged into a nearby river from an upriver hospital, would have a private right of action against the hospital for violating her rights to clean water. A court could award the beachgoer monetary damages and issue a restraining order against the hospital forbidding further discharges.

When an individual lives on a river or stream, she is entitled to clean water from the river or stream flowing through her private real property. Thus, an upstream dweller is not entitled to discharge any matter into the river or stream to render the downstream water unclean. Urinating, one time, into the Mississippi River, would not cause a problem for a landowner one mile downstream. Discharging household waste into a small neighborhood stream would be a violation of the downstream property owners' rights to clean water. Between these two extremes, a court would have to decide those discharges which are not violations of rights and those which are.

These examples will suffice for our present purposes. As stated, the details of this "Leave No Trace Behind" solution will be complex. The common law will define the rules.

One can see that polluters would not long remain polluters with thousands of potential individual litigants chaffing at the bit to sue, to say nothing of the Sierra Club or Earth First! There would be no need for the Environmental Protection Agency (EPA) in these circumstances. (Leviathan EPA is a superorganism whose demise would be welcomed by Fabian Libertarians.)

The general principle is "Leave No Trace Behind" on other people's property or upon the commons. Each of us owns our own stuff, but we are not entitled to allow our stuff, including our waste products, to interfere with another's use of his stuff or of the commons (the biosphere).

Land Viewed as "Commons"

We do not wish to imply that anything goes on private real property (land) so long as there is no impact on adjacent landowners. One must consider later landowners in the chain of title. No one lives forever. Real property is bought, sold, gifted, transferred, and inherited.

A person is entitled to buy a brand-new automobile and destroy it immediately, provided the residue is properly disposed. Such is the nature of private *personal* property. We own it. We can destroy it. Of course, who would want to? We can imagine that the new car owner is a movie producer who wants to use his brand-new car in the chase scene of her action-adventure movie.

Land, though, exists forever and is limited in quantity. It is bad public policy to allow a private land owner to permanently render "her" land unusable, since it will not be "her" land for eternity or even beyond her lifetime. The most obvious permanent ruination of land is the storage upon it of nuclear waste material. Even if the presence of nuclear waste material on land is not a threat to adjacent property owners, the destruction of the plot of land for any other use for 240,000 years is bad public policy. Greenpeace claims that plutonium 239 has a half-life of 24,000 years and will remain hazardous for 240,000 years.

Technology may well solve the problem of nuclear waste disposal. An obvious, though expensive, solution is to blast the nuclear waste by rocket into the sun. Other less expensive solutions are almost certainly to be discovered by science.

The general principle ought to be that the use and abuse of private real property has no bounds except: (1) the use cannot threaten adjacent land owners, and (2) the abuse can be mitigated for a price less than the value of the land. The principle for exception 2 is that a landowner ought not to destroy forever the value of "her" land on the grounds that it will not always be "hers." In this sense, viewed from the perspective of centuries, real property (land) is in the commons. Therefore, a large tract of land might be used for a junkyard as the "junk" has value and can be removed from the land and sold or recycled, returning the land to its "unabused" state. More problematical is a landfill. While a landfill might be mitigated and returned to its original state, the cost to do so is likely to be much higher than the value of the land. The "half-life" of a landfill is likely to be millennia. The landowner might collect a storage/mitigation fee from his customers to permit the use as landfill and avoid litigation.

Conclusion to "Leave No Trace Behind"

In summary, Libertarians believe in both freedom and responsibility. Part of responsibility includes not allowing the exercise of his freedom to impair another's exercise of her freedom. Recall the freedom is simply the protection of private property rights by the rule of law. The radical conclusion we draw from these Libertarian assumptions is that one ought not to despoil the biosphere or land in the commons. Even private *real* property (land) when viewed from the perspective of centuries is in the commons.

Chapter 11—Abortion

No opinion should be held with fervour. No one holds with fervour that seven times eight is fifty-six, because it can be known that this is the case. Fervour is only necessary in commending an opinion which is doubtful or demonstrably false.

—Bertrand Russell

Cover for Leviathan

"Divide and conquer." No issue provides better cover for Leviathan than the issue of abortion. Abortion is about life and death at the margins. Everybody believes that murder is evil. Murder is the unlawful killing with malice aforethought of another "human being." What is a "human being" at the margins for the purposes of the definition of murder is debatable. A barely living human vegetable at the extreme of old age, ravaged with incurable disease, racked with pain but for large doses of morphine, unable to eat or drink on his own, without the possibility of consciousness, without any hope of recovery, hooked up to machines for medicine, fluids, nourishment, and excretion is at one margin. Some social conservatives would fight bitterly to keep such a person plugged into his machines to be kept alive in a living Hell. Recall the tragic Terri Schiavo case from Florida in 2005.[54] A sperm swimming upstream in utero toward a waiting human ovum is at the other margin. Catholic doctrine forbids birth control. Many Americans do not take this "moral" doctrine seriously.[55]

Leviathan Big Government exists for life and more life, money, and power. Leviathan cares not one wit about human life. Lacking consciousness and therefore a conscience, Leviathan is by definition a sociopath. Private family decisions at the margins of life do not concern Leviathan at all. However, Leviathan benefits from the ***abortion wars*** because the hysterical and relentless fighting of well-intentioned people about the margins keeps the slaves of Leviathan Big Government thoroughly ***distracted*** from the evil of Leviathan. A great result for Leviathan.

For some people engaged in the abortion debate, a political candidate's position on abortion (for or against) is the only issue that matters. These are one-issue voters. No candidate will be supported who does not agree with the abortion advocate (either "for" or "against"). Both sides can be fanatical.

Fabian Libertarians need to work on abortion fanatics to get them to prioritize American Freedom over all other political issues. Freedom is the protection of property rights by the rule of law. Issues at the margin are of lesser importance than the core principle of protection of property rights. ***The right to life is the core property right.*** Whether the old, sick, and cruelly suffering human described above has a "life" to be protected by the rule of law is a question at the margin! Whether a human sperm swimming upstream in utero has a "life" to be protected by the rule of law is a question at the margin!

One does not have to give up the margin, but let us secure the center first. Secure the right to property at the core first! Worry about the margins when the core is secure.

This chapter attempts to explain some of the hysteria in the abortion debate, hoping to bring some of the fanatics back to the core of the fight for American Freedom. We can leave the margins for another day.

Bertrand Russell suggests that fervor about an opinion is present only when the opinion "is doubtful or demonstrably false." *Both* sides of the abortion issue are commonly held and publicly expressed with fervor. One might therefore conclude that both sides of the abortion issue are *doubtful*. (Both sides cannot be *demonstrably false* under the law of the excluded middle, which states that only a proposition or its negation can be true.) Questions at the margins are notoriously fraught with doubt.[56]

How are we to survive the existence of doubt? Mature adults realize that doubt is omnipresent in our lives and cannot be avoided.

Here is an analysis of the abortion issue which will help the would-be Fabian Libertarian politician.

Scratch a Zealot and Find a Sinner

The emotional stakes in the abortion debate are rarely discussed. These emotional stakes are a major confounding factor in the debates. Identifying these emotional factors will be useful.

The Pro-*Choice* Zealot

Some people who argue in favor of and against abortion are highly invested in the matter. The investment we are talking about is some *personal experience* with abortion.

If we hypothesize that the highly emotional pro-choice person has had an abortion, her high level of emotion is explained. A pro-choice person who has had an abortion cannot allow herself to consider the idea that abortion is wrong because there is *no redemption for murder*. (We do not think abortion is murder. We are saying that the pro-choice zealot may have a repressed belief that abortion is murder.) A person who commits murder cannot make it right. A life once taken cannot be restored. Some people who have had an abortion are, at the root, arguing about whether they have committed an unforgivable sin—not exactly a topic of conversation to be taken lightly.

A man who has encouraged his partner to have an abortion might also be unable to allow himself to consider the idea that abortion is wrong.

A person who has had an abortion **can** enter into the abortion debate, but as a matter of intellectual fairness, she should not exhibit a highly emotional state during the debate or allow her high emotions to affect her reasoning. There are two ways she might accomplish this. First, she can thoroughly and completely analyze her decision to have had an abortion and arrive at a moral certainty that her decision was correct. She can thus engage in the abortion debate as a philosopher and a teacher with no fear of the forthcoming contrary arguments. She will know she has already thought through all the questions and answers. Second, she may have philosopher-like powers and be capable of setting aside the risks to her psychological well-being posed by engaging in a debate in which she might learn that her decision to have a abortion was, by her own newly informed judgment, morally wrong. The capacity to set aside real threats to one's ego for the sake of the truth requires extraordinary moral courage. Any person who exhibits high emotion during the abortion debate lacks this capacity. A person is unwise, generally, to engage in a debate with a person who has an obviously high emotional stake in the outcome.

The Pro-*Life* Zealot

Atonement

On the pro-life side of the debate, there are also those who are highly emotional. Consider again a woman who has had an abortion. This time, though, she is highly emotional about her **pro-*life*** position. She may have decided that she has committed a sin that may not be redeemed or forgiven. In an effort to seek redemption anyway, she may have become a "zealot for life." It is hard to live with guilt. One way to live with guilt is to live a life of atonement. Proselytizing the pro-life message can be, for some, a life of atonement.

A man who has encouraged his partner to have an abortion might also be seeking redemption having concluded that abortion is wrong. He might seek atonement by ferociously proselytizing the pro-life message.

Anthropomorphization

Some males who participate in the abortion debate are highly emotional. In fact, *male* pro-lifers seem to dominate the public debate. The emotional intensity of these men is baffling. They, after all, can never have had an abortion though they may have participated by encouraging their partner to have an abortion. In trying to understand highly emotional male pro-lifers, we might look to our own emotions about the violation of the rights of adult human beings for clues. Almost everyone, for example, is able to understand getting highly emotional about the murder of an adult human being.

We find it difficult to watch the beginning of movies that contain acts of murder and mayhem to motivate the story. We are able to imagine ourselves in the place of such a victim. We can project how he might feel. We can experience his rage, his sense of loss, and his sense of injustice at the evil, early, and violent ending of his own life. We can *empathize* with his suffering. This emotional identification with others is at the root of the outrage we feel at the violation of the rights of others.

Consider animal-rights zealots. Such a person engages in the same process of identification with an animal. He puts himself in the position of a dog being sacrificed, for example, in order to train a surgeon, and the animal-rights zealot is horrified. This identification involves an anthropomorphization of the animal. (In order to understand why animals are used to train heart surgeons, the animal-rights zealot might imagine himself or a loved one under the skilled hands of a heart surgeon whose surgical mastery derives from thirty heart operations upon animals during the surgeon's medical training.)

The highly emotional male pro-lifer may derive his strong emotional reaction against abortion in the same manner as the animal-rights activist—by anthropomorphization of the human zygote, embryo, or fetus. Perhaps we are not satisfied by introspection that the emotion experienced by the pro-lifer for an aborted fetus comes from a personal identification with the fetus (as happens when we empathize with adult humans whose rights are violated). What then is another possible explanation of a highly emotional commitment to the pro-life position?

Children Are Sacred

Children are sacred. In fact, children are the most sacred beings on earth. Most parents cannot imagine the nonexistence of their children. They cannot even *allow* their minds to go there. Most parents cannot conceive of themselves surviving the premature death of a child. Spiritually, many parents could **not** survive such a death.

Evidence of the status of children as the Number One sacred value on earth is to be found everywhere, including politics. Consider the classic image of the politician kissing the baby or the political untouchability of government schools or the title of many legislative proposals along the lines of the "Save the Children Act of 2021" often having very little to do with children or with saving them. If a politician claims his program will "Save the Children," it cannot be criticized. Outside of politics, parents' lives are dedicated to the care and maintenance of their children.

The bloom of the protective zone around our sacred children is almost infinite. As in the case of the "Save the Children Act of 2021," the protection is often ineffectual or even irrational.

Perhaps the most highly emotional male pro-lifers derive the intensity of their emotion against abortion from the infinite value they appropriately assign to their own children. The zealot identifies the human zygote, the human embryo, and the human fetus within the body of a stranger *with the zealot's own living child*. Like the anthropomorphization of animals by animal-rights activists, this identification of a human zygote, embryo, and fetus with a living child is questionable. Because the identification of an early stage fetus with a living child is, in fact, weak, the abortion debate focuses on the so-called "partial birth abortion." This procedure is allegedly the in utero killing of a late-term fetus or fully formed human child. At this stage the identification of the very-late-term fetus with a living child is strong.

Summarizing the Emotional Issues

In summary, identification of the source of the excessively high emotions involved in the abortion debate is important to those who are interested in discovering the philosophical truth of the matter. Philosophical truth is to be distinguished from emotional states. People often bring certain emotional states *to* the debate. These emotional truths must be identified and *set aside* while reasoning. A person who, for emotional reasons, cannot *allow* her mind to admit the known alternatives to a philosophic question should not engage in a debate about the subject. No reasonable person should engage such a person in the debate since, for private emotional reasons of one of the parties, the outcome is predetermined.

A person who, having had an abortion, defends abortion rights because she cannot tolerate labeling herself a murderer is not interested in truth, but in not labeling herself a murderer. A person who is pro-life because she feels she has committed an unpardonable sin (in her own mind) for having had an abortion and must atone for it by being pro-life is not interested in truth, but in seeking redemption. A pro-life person who mentally equates his own sacred children with a human zygote, embryo, or fetus in the body of a stranger is not interested in truth, but in defending the lives of his own children.

A person interested in truth must be willing to follow all leads wherever they may go, even if he does not like the results. If his goal is to preserve his predebate emotions about the facts, he must forego reason, stick to faith, avoid or repress the issue entirely, or, as is most often the case, be irrational and ferocious. Reason, to be reason, must be impartial. Facts exist independently of our feelings.

The Politics of Abortion

Having identified the intense emotions that accompany the abortion debate and vowed to set them aside for the sake of truth, let us consider the politics of the subject. Considering politics before ethics (which will be addressed at the end of this chapter) may seem like putting the cart before the horse, since politics depends upon ethics. However, there are reasons for considering the politics of abortion before the ethics of abortion. First, one can derive a proper politics without first determining the morality of abortion. In other words, the *general* principles of politics can be made clear without even addressing the *particular* ethics of abortion. The second reason for considering the politics of abortion first is that the political issue is easier than the moral question. So, what are our political principles?

Aristotle observes that man is the rational animal. The human being's essential means of survival is her rational faculty. This rational faculty exists only in the individual. If a human being is to survive, she must use her rational faculty. Stated another way as a normative expression, a human being *should* use her rational faculty. This principle that woman should use her rational faculty applies even when a woman is among women, that is, in society. The philosophy of reason holds that **rights are conditions of man's existence in society**. In other words, it is of value to a human being to live in society, but only on certain conditions. For life in society to be of value to a human being, he must have the right to life. He must have a *moral claim* enforceable by government that he be allowed to live. For life in society to be of value to a human being, he must be free to act upon his judgment, that is, to use his mind, his means of survival, in the material realm. For life in society to be of value to a human being, he must be free to act upon his judgment in the spiritual realm. If life is to be of value to a human being, he must have the right to keep the product of his labor. These are the rights to life, liberty, the pursuit of happiness, and property.

The important part of the definition of rights in the context of abortion is "in society." Rights are conditions of man's existence *in society*. Clearly, a woman and the one-celled zygote within her are not a society and the concept of rights does not apply. Clearly, a woman and her newborn baby are a society of two and the concept of rights does apply. Between zygote and newborn baby there is a process of change or becoming during which the woman's ownership right to her own body gives way to the augmenting rights of the developing fetus. ***A line must be drawn to define these rights***. Government must draw this line using reason (not popular vote or public opinion polls).

The United States Supreme Court in its decision in *Roe v. Wade*, 410 U.S. 113 (1973), has done a brilliant job of analyzing the biological process of becoming, weighing the interests of state, mother and fetus, and providing a rational solution to the political question. This chapter cannot add to the analysis of that august body and we refer the reader to the court's most excellent opinion. The court concludes, generally, that during the first trimester of pregnancy no regulation of abortion is permitted; during the second trimester regulations designed to protect the woman's health are permitted; and during the third trimester, when the fetus is viable, abortion may be prohibited if the life or health of the mother is not at stake.

The Ethics of Abortion

Morality is a personal tool for survival. Morality is necessary because we do not automatically know what is right and because we are not infallible. Because we have volition and because we are not infallible, we need principles to guide our choices and actions. The guiding principle of morality is man's life *as a man* as opposed to the life of a carrot, a lion, a beggar, a liar or a thief. Thus, morality depends upon a view of man. Aristotle's view is that man is the rational animal and that man survives by creating things like food, shelter, clothing, and software. The normative "ought" is a conditional "ought" of this form—if man is to survive as a man, then he "ought" to be rational and to produce goods.

The penalties for acting immorally are imposed by reality (*internal* and external) and by other people. The most common penalty imposed upon an immoral person by others is avoidance, shunning. The penalties imposed by reality range from unhappiness to death. For example, it is immoral not to support oneself if one is able. The penalty for not having a productive purpose is, at a minimum, unhappiness. This penalty is imposed by the nonproductive individual's *internal* reality. If a nonproductive individual does not have others who are willing to insulate him from reality, he will starve to death. This penalty is imposed by external reality. Another example: it is immoral to avoid thinking about problems by remaining drunk all the time. The penalty for being a drunk all the time is unhappiness, illness and, eventually, death.

Note that if one is not merely immoral, but violates the rights of others, the government will impose fines or imprisonment as a consequence.

Reality includes an *internal* reality, a psychological reality. The individual's appraisal of himself is part of reality. A person *cannot* be happy without self-esteem. The reason most of us do not commit fraud or theft or murder is not fear of arrest and punishment, but fear of the judgment of our own minds. A healthy mind cannot live with the guilt of murder, for example.

Because of the potential for *self-punishment*, it is extremely important to be clear when deciding to terminate a pregnancy.

We said that reasoning about the morality of abortion was more complex than reasoning about the politics of abortion. Part of the reason that political reasoning is easier than moral reasoning is that the Supreme Court of the United States has already done a magnificent job of political reasoning. We can simply read the court's opinion and evaluate it. However, the most important reason that the ethics of abortion are so much more difficult than the politics of abortion is that the variables are many and in combination the variables result in ***thousands of different moral problems***. Among the categories of the variables are the circumstances of the pregnancy, the values of the pregnant woman, the health of the woman, the duration of the pregnancy, and the health of the fetus. The circumstances of the pregnancy can vary from incest or rape of a child to pregnancy chosen by a mature married couple after years of thought and study. The values of the woman are determined by her age, her life circumstances, her intelligence, her moral training, and the thinking she has done or failed to do. Depending upon the health of the woman, her pregnancy might be likely to kill her or to present no unusual threat to her physical well-being. Depending upon the duration of the pregnancy, the entity to be aborted can vary from a one-celled zygote to a fully formed, though in utero, human child. The health of the entity to be aborted might be such that it has no possibility of coming to term or of surviving birth by more than a few weeks or the entity might be perfect and capable, if allowed to come to term, of living a long, happy and healthy life. ***These variables can be combined into literally thousands of moral questions.***

Two Ethical Examples at the Extremes

Here are two relatively simple questions at the extremes: (1) Is it moral for a thirteen-year-old virgin, the victim of a violent rape by her father, to voluntarily ingest a day-after pill to insure that she does not become pregnant by the rapist? The easy answer is "Yes." (2) Is it moral for a mature married couple who have decided after a long marriage, much thought, and study to terminate their intentional pregnancy in the eighteenth week of pregnancy because they have learned by DNA testing their perfect fetus is a girl and they wanted a boy? The easy answer is "No."

While these two extreme cases are "obvious," they may not be obvious to everyone. Therefore, let us do the moral analysis.

Case One

Proposition: It is moral for a thirteen-year-old virgin, the victim of a violent rape by her father, to voluntarily ingest a day-after pill to insure that she does not become pregnant by the rapist. The moral analysis begins by identifying the facts of the case, specifically in the categories of variables previously mentioned. These variables are the circumstances of the pregnancy, the values of the pregnant woman, the health of the woman, the duration of the pregnancy, and the health of the fetus.

The circumstances of the pregnancy are deliberately chosen to be the worst case imaginable. Not only is the girl violated, but also she is violated by the person from whom she has a right to expect the greatest love, concern, and protectiveness. She is now likely to be without a father during an important stage in her life, because, among other reasons, the rapist, the victim's father, will be in prison for rape. She is physically and psychologically traumatized and will never be psychologically whole, though one hopes she may someday with appropriate therapy be able to achieve some level of happiness. She is unable financially to support a resulting child. She is incapable of forming a bond to the baby because of the circumstances of the conception and because of her own youth and psychological trauma.

The values of our thirteen-year-old incest victim are those of any adolescent—her appearance, her social standing among her friends, achieving independence from her parents, and her school work. As a rape victim, she will be attaching a high value to overcoming the psychological trauma of the rape and the most profound betrayal that a child can endure. A potential baby is *not* among her values.

The health of our thirteen-year-old victim is also threatened by the potential pregnancy. Medically speaking, a young adolescent faces higher health risks due to pregnancy than a mature woman does.

The duration of the pregnancy is the shortest possible conceivable. There may be no fertilization at the moment of ingestion of the morning-after pill. Or there may be only a zygote within her or an embryo of very few cells.

The health of the zygote of this adolescent mother is at greater risk. Because a conception in this case is the result of incest, the risk of birth defects is higher than normal. The mother's young age is a factor that increases risk of health problems for this zygote.

The consideration of all five categories of variables leads us to conclude that there is every reason to abort in this case and no reason to endure the pregnancy. The reader should not be tempted to change the facts. **Do not be tempted**, for example, to hypothesize that the child victim wants to have her own father's child. That is a possible case, but it is not the case we are analyzing here. It is another one of the thousands of moral questions that might be presented to a pregnant woman. We are only offering an extreme case to show the process of reasoning about it.

Case Two

Proposition: It is immoral for a mature married couple who have decided after a long marriage, much thought and study to terminate their intentional pregnancy in the *eighteenth* week of pregnancy because they have learned by DNA testing their perfect fetus is a girl and they wanted a boy. Again we begin our moral analysis by considering the five categories of variables.

The circumstances of the pregnancy in this case are ideal. The parents are emotionally, morally, and legally committed to one another. They have chosen to have a child. They are ready, willing, and able to have a child.

The values of the parents are, with one exception, ideal. The parents have chosen parenthood for this time in their lives.

The health of a fully grown, mature woman in her prime childbearing years is not abnormally threaten by pregnancy.

The length of the pregnancy is eighteen weeks, in the second trimester. Pregnancy normally lasts thirty-eight weeks. While incapable of living outside the mother's womb, this fetus is well on her way to life.

The health of the fetus as determined by DNA testing is perfect.

The consideration of all five categories of variables leads to the conclusion that there is every reason to give birth to this girl fetus and no reason to abort. The preference for a boy is not sufficient to outweigh all the other factors in favor of life for the fetus. Many medical professionals would be unwilling to perform an abortion for this couple. If she does get an abortion in these circumstances and if the facts were to become known, she would be shunned by some people. If the facts were not discovered, she might experience a lifetime of guilt for her act.

A reader might be tempted to ask, is it wrong to want a boy or a girl baby? Of course not. What is wrong about the couple in this extreme example is the place in their hierarchy of values that they assign to the boy-girl preference. An eighteen-week fetus is not like an automobile that might be purchased or not depending upon its color. Unlike car ownership, parenthood is a *sacred* human activity. It is an individual's only opportunity to experience him or herself as a god—as a creator of life and as an object of worship. The love that parents experience for their children is ***inexpressible*** and ***incomprehensible*** to nonparents. Parenthood alone is sufficient to provide meaning to life. In the full context of the value that is parenthood, the sex of the eighteenth-week fetus is of no importance. To forego the greatest human adventure at eighteen weeks for reason of the sex of the fetus is unthinkable. A person who would undergo an abortion for this reason has a terribly distorted value system.[57]

The Astonishing Presumption of Pro-lifers

Between these admittedly extreme hypothetical cases of abortion are ***thousands of very hard moral questions***. The presumption of pro-lifers to proclaim ***their*** right(?) to decide by law all such questions ***for a pregnant woman*** is astonishing. Within the parameters of *Roe v. Wade*, the pregnant woman must make the decision to abort or not. **The moral decision is hers alone.** If she makes a moral error, the only penalty (assuming her error is not made public) will be the judgment she ***imposes upon herself***. Because this penalty can be severe (a lifetime of guilt), utmost caution and reflection is called for in the choice of sexual partner, in the decision to have sex at all, and in the decision to terminate a pregnancy.

Conclusion on Abortion

Fabian Libertarians on the federal level ought to stay clear of this issue, whichever side she takes, pro-life or pro-choice. On the state level, the Fabian Libertarian needs to make clear that the issue of abortion ***ought not*** to *be* "high" on the political "things to do" list. Secure the core of property rights first. Worry about the margins later.

Chapter 12—Conclusion

Wednesday, January 20, 2117, is our target date, Presidential Inauguration Day 2117. On that day a Fabian Libertarian candidate for president of the United States will take the oath of office. A Fabian Libertarian majority Congress will be in place. The new American Renaissance will be thoroughly underway.

One Hundred Years: Not So Long a Time

After the invasion of Italy by Carthaginian general Hannibal in 218 BC, it was not until seventy-two years later in 146 BC at the end of the Third Punic War that Carthage was finally destroyed by Rome. Our hero Fabius Maximus was fifty-seven years dead by that time.

To many readers, especially young people, one hundred years seems like a long time. Consider though that the Libertarian Party of the United States was founded on December 11, 1971, forty-five years ago as of 2016. The Libertarian Party today can claim that the American public is generally aware of Libertarian principles. There is even a Libertarian wing of the Republican Party. Dozens of politicians and celebrities identify themselves as Libertarians.[58]

To date the Libertarian Party has not enjoyed much success in electing actual "Libertarian" candidates to public office. Our Fabian Libertarian one-hundred-years plan will gradually improve on this record.

We can expect to advance slowly at first, state house district by state house district, and then state by state, and finally to national offices. When we show our first successes in state house races, other freedom-minded young people will rally to our effort and remarkable progress can be expected.

We predict that the first Fabian Libertarian candidates will be elected to the state House of Representatives within ten years. Ten more Fabian Libertarian candidates will be elected to the state House of Representatives within twenty years. At that point, other state Libertarian Parties will imitate our successes.

During our one-hundred-years fight for American Freedom, our current Socialist America will not remain politically static. We can expect that the Socialist juggernaut currently crushing the American economy and American Freedom **will be slowed**. The Old Socialists will begin to question the wisdom of their political choices. The parents of Flint, Michigan, whose children were drinking lead-laced tap water in 2015 supplied by their Leviathan Big Government, are, hopefully, beginning to question their Socialistic choices. The American political environment will slowly improve over the next one hundred years as a result of Fabian Libertarian efforts.

The Great Depression II

As was suggested in chapter 3 on economics, Leviathan Big Government causes and perpetuates depressions. By the year 2021 and maybe as soon as 2017, the world will know that we are in the Great Depression II. A depression is caused by a massive misallocation of resources. The symptoms of the depression are the stopping of work in the misallocated economic zones and the reallocation of capital and human resources into new, more productive economic zones. Leviathan Big Government does everything in its power ***to thwart*** the stopping of work in the misallocated economic zones and the reallocation of capital and human resources into new, more productive economic zones.

We provided an example of a localized depression involving real estate in America from 2007 to present caused by the Community Reinvestment Act (CRA) of 1977. The CRA encouraged financial institutions to loan money for residential housing to people who could not afford to repay, resulting in a housing bubble that burst in 2007. Housing prices plummeted. Businesses went bankrupt. Many people today are "inverted" on their homes, meaning that their mortgage debt exceeds the fair market value of their homes.

Leviathan Big Government has, for the last decade, been pumping money into American economy to **hide the fact of wide-spread deflation**. The collapse of the price of oil is merely one example of the current worldwide deflation. When people discover that resources have been misallocated, the prices of the assets to which the resources were misallocated will collapse. **Leviathan Big Government's job is to hide this reality.**

The hiding of asset misallocation cannot remain successful forever. America's public debt is acknowledged to be over 17 trillion dollars or $55,630 per capita. This debt will never be repaid. This Federal Government debt is exactly like the unfunded pension promises made by bankrupt municipalities, states, and countries, that can never be paid in current dollars. Paper money can be printed by Leviathan Big Government to "pay" these debts nominally.

America's actual debt is certainly in excess of 100 trillion dollars taking into consideration the many unfunded promises to pay for things such as Social Security, Medicare, and Medicaid.

This American economic house of cards will start falling down sometime within the next five years. The Great Depression II will be recognized by all. The political party in power will be blamed. That political party will not be the Libertarian Party.

The solution to a Great Depression is bankruptcy. Declare the enterprise dead, the debt cancelled, and start over. Most people's savings will be destroyed. However, everyone can resume working in areas of the economy not involving the assets to which resources were misallocated. The sharply devalued assets can be sold in bankruptcy and used productively by their new owners. An economic boom would follow within months of total liquidation.

A return to the gold standard for money is necessary. The first step is to remove Leviathan Big Government's monopoly on the creation of money. Entrepreneurs would be free to create other stores of value, such as Bitcoin. People suspicious of new money can use gold and silver coins, ubiquitous even nowadays. Certainly, storage warehouses for gold and silver would be created and those warehouses could issue "deposit receipts" for the gold and silver in the warehouse that could be used as money. As with all economic problems, we and the would-be Socialist Central Planners **lack the imagination** to foresee the dozens of great solutions to economic problems that the seven billion people in the world will invent.

Another problem of money is all the worthless paper that the United States government has printed, not only paper money, but also promissory notes, like treasury bills, notes, and bonds. One solution, perhaps the only solution, is bankruptcy. Simply declare that all paper money and the promissory notes of the United States shall be redeemed for the existing assets of the United States. This is what happens to an individual in chapter 7 bankruptcy. The individual's assets are sold by the bankruptcy trustee and paid to the creditors. The individual's debts are extinguished.

Leviathan Big Government owns 85 percent of Nevada and 47 percent of all the land in the western United States.[59] Leviathan Big Government owns many valuable buildings and other assets. All Leviathan Big Government assets should be declared equal in value to all of the claims against Leviathan Big Government. The assets should be given in discharge of the claims. After that, Leviathan Big Government should be out of the business of printing or borrowing money forever.

Of course, this proposed solution will never be tolerated by Leviathan Big Government. Instead, Leviathan Big Government will print as much money as necessary to hide asset deflation, to bail out its Leviathan Big Buddies, and to repay the government debts in inflated, worthless dollars. Leviathan Big Government will allow the world economy to collapse. To understand what collapse looks like, consider Detroit, Michigan, or Eastern Europe during the Cold War. During the collapse, Leviathan Big Government clamor for ever more power.

Fabian Libertarians need to be wary during the Great Depression II. Calls for more Totalitarian Government will reach extremes.

The Invention of Freedom

The Fabian Libertarian assumption is that we Americans can choose to be free. Whether we can ***will***, as in ***an act of will***, American Freedom into existence remains to be seen. The other possibility is the freedom arises from certain social-geographic circumstances.

The City-State

Freedom began in ancient Greece (800–300 BC). Most of the credit for freedom goes to Ancient Athens. The documents describing and philosophizing about freedom were composed there. The wisdom of the ancient Greeks contained in those ancient Greek writings was rediscovered during the European Renaissance. The ancient Greek wisdom was transmitted to prerevolutionary America from Europe. Our founding fathers followed the ancient Greek example in founding America. Thus was born American Freedom. Unfortunately, the lessons of the Jean-Jacques Rousseau, Father of Democratic Totalitarianism, came shortly thereafter to America leading to our present crisis of Socialism.

The question is: Did the Greeks invent freedom *ex nihilo* or were the Greeks free because of certain social-geographic circumstances?

There was a great trauma that destroyed the area around the Aegean Sea (between modern-day Greece and Turkey) prior to 800 BC, leading to a Dark Ages. Over the centuries, from the Greek Dark Ages forward, hard individuals took up farming in mountainous, rocky, and otherwise inhospitable Greek terrain. Common farm products included grapevines and olive trees. Both of these products require careful, individualized attention. Olive trees require twenty years to produce fruit and bear fruit only once every two years. Grapevines require special care as well. A small farm in ancient Greece required careful, individualized cultivation over decades by a specialized individual called the yeoman farmer.

Compare a small Greek farm with the great river valleys of the Tigris-Euphrates River and the Nile River. In these river basins, annual flooding inundated vast land areas, providing rich soil for immense crops of wheat and barley. These large fertile plains were suitable for large populations of farmworkers performing routine work, not requiring special expertise.

River-valley farming is ideal for slavery. Farming an inhospitable mountainside is ideal for the free man. Pharaoh cannot leash by the neck enough yeoman farmers, experts at cultivating vines and trees, feed them, and have anything left over for Pharaoh. Should Pharaoh determine to kill the leashed yeoman farmer, who would replace the farming expert willing to work and plan over decades? A slave with a hoe is endlessly replaceable by Pharaoh.

The great enemy of the ancient Greeks was Ancient Persia of the Tigris-Euphrates River valley. The ancient Greeks represent Western Freedom. The ancient Persians represent Slavery and Totalitarianism. We all remember the famous Battle of Thermopylae (480 BC), in which three hundred Spartans, led by Spartan King Leonidas, held back for three days the Persian hordes of Xerxes I. The battle pits free men against slaves.

A yeoman farmer has a one-on-one relationship with reality, with the weather, with the terrain, with his crops, with his animals, with disease, with wild animals, with irascible neighbors, and with brigands. The yeoman and his small family group work their privately owned farm far from Pharaoh or other pretenders to dictatorship. **The yeoman farmer is by circumstance of lifestyle and geography free.**

Overtime, the yeoman farmer determined that having a citadel to which his family might retreat in times of war and having capable neighbors willing to fight common foes was life-preserving. The yeoman farmer would meet with his capable neighbors in the citadel, now called a polis, to discuss important issues, including defense of their farms. Thus, democracy was born.

When the yeoman farmers met as a body and voted to go to war, **they themselves** donned personal armor and picked up their personal weapons and fought together with their neighbors in a phalanx. It is thus that the yeoman became farmer, citizens, and soldier. This ideal of farmer, citizen, and soldier is the idea at the root of Western Freedom, at the root of American Freedom.

The political theorizing of century following the golden age of Athens was **a description of freedom rather than the invention of freedom.**

The question stated above: "Did the Greeks invent freedom *ex nihilo* or were the Greeks free because of certain social-geographic circumstances?" The answer is: The Greeks were free because of certain social-geographic circumstances.

Are Not We All on Pharaoh's Leash?

Let us be honest. Are not most of us the slaves of Pharaoh and do not most of us approve? The life of a yeoman farmer is not easy. Going *mano a mano* with nature is not an American Socialists idea of fun. The cradle to grave Socialism which it is our pleasure(?) to enjoy these days is happily embraced by the great majority of Americans. Go back to the Introduction and review the list of Fabian Socialist essays written in the early twentieth century. The Socialist wish list is accomplished.

Our problem, as we have stated several times before, is that **we lack the imagination** to foresee the world in which we would live under American Freedom. Good economic analysis requires that we consider all the consequences of an economic policy. We can only see the immediate consequence of our personal government benefit being cut (there are thousands of instances). None of us, other than Steven Jobs, founder of Apple, could have imagined the consequences of the invention of the iPhone. None of us can see the actual consequences of Leviathan Big Government's substantial ***arrest of human economic activity.***

Every one of the seven billion people in the world is constantly striving to improve her condition. She is looking for economies, ways to save money, and ways to improve her productivity. The cumulative effect of these efforts is constantly increasing productivity, constantly dropping prices, and constantly increasing standards of living for everyone.

Can you imagine what life would be like without our tablet technologies (iPhone, iPad, Android tablets, and so on), had Leviathan Big Government anticipated the rocketlike progress and outlawed it for the sake of its Leviathan Big Buddies whose businesses were to be disrupted by the new technologies? You had better believe that every business bankrupted by new technologies would in retrospect have demanded that Leviathan Big Government stop the competition. Remember Leviathan Big Government's efforts to thwart Uber and Airbnb.com. Remember the Luddite Fallacy that new technology destroys jobs.

Leviathan Big Government would freeze all economic activity in place if it could get away with it politically. *Atlas Shrugged* (1957) by

Ayn Rand (1905–1982) fictionalizes an attempt to freeze all economic activity with an executive order entitled Directive 10-289.

Fabian Libertarians dream of living in a world in which all the people of the world (seven billion good people at present) are set free to make improvements in their lives that will, of necessity, improve the standard of living of all.

Movement as the Cause of Freedom

Freedom makes occasional appearances on earth. Freedom occurs in first full flower in ancient Greece. Freedom occurs in last full flower around the time of revolutionary America. There are echoes of freedom across time and around the world. Freedom, remember, is the societal condition in which property rights are protected by the rule of law. In ancient Greece, the fundamental property unit was the yeoman's farm. In revolutionary America, the fundamental property unit was the family farm.

We have just argued that freedom arose in ancient Greece because of the social and geographic circumstances of the yeoman farmer. Another theory of freedom is that freedom is a consequence of the ability to move away from the tyrant or the would-be tyrant.

There were thousands of Greek colonies around the Mediterranean Sea during the times of ancient Greece. From the western edge of the Mediterranean Sea in Spain to the far eastern edge of the Black Sea, from the north at Marseille, France, to the south in Egypt, the Greeks settled autonomous colonies. Each of these colonies was a *polis*, an autonomous city-state with a defensive perimeter. The reasons for the founding of these colonies were as numerous as the colonies themselves. People do not generally pack up and leave their homes without a good reason. One reason for disaffection is being restrained from enacting your free will. **People move in order to be free**. People move away from would-be tyrants. Upon arrival at the new colony, the colonists set up and operate their new family farms.

This theory states that the ancient Greeks were free because **they could move away** from their mother cities to new colonies that would be ruled by the colonists and not by the mother city.

When Europeans arrived in Jamestown, Virginia, in 1607, a vast continent remained to be discovered. The settlement of the continental United States was completed in 1890,[60] 283 years later. The movement of the American settlers across the continental United States occurred for reasons analogous to the creation of new ancient Greek colonies. As we stated above, **people move in order to be free.**

This theory states that Americans were free because **they could move away** from their former settlements to new frontier settlements that would be ruled by the settlers and not by the government of the former settlements.

Now America is full, and there are no new places to which to move. People, of course, move from less free states to more free states these days. People are moving from Detroit, Michigan, if they can. People are moving from Flint, Michigan, if they can. People are moving from the northeastern states to the south, if they can. People are moving from California to Colorado and Texas, if they can.

Such interstate moves are only marginally effective because many of the movers are Socialists and they carry their economy destroying ideas with them, thus hastening the rush of the relatively freer state to complete Socialism.

Freedom as an Act of the Will

We know what freedom looks like by the examples of ancient Greece and revolutionary America. The question is: In the absence of the social-geographic circumstances present in ancient Greece and in revolutionary America, can we restore American Freedom?

The only answer is: We have to try. In the absence of the social (yeoman farmers) and geographic (inhospitable, isolated farms and the ability to move away from tyrants) factors, we must employ *education* as our main tool to restore American Freedom. People must be *educated* about ancient Greece and revolutionary America. We must provide our children with a Classical Education in history, literature, and philosophy. A classical education is the teaching of the Great Books, including these:

- *The Iliad* by Homer
- The Odyssey by Homer
- The great Greek plays of Aeschylus, Euripides, Sophocles, and Aristophanes

- The Peloponnesian War by Thucydides
- The works of Plato, including *The Republic*
- The works of Aristotle, including the *Nicomachean Ethics*
- Plutarch's *Lives of Famous Greeks and Romans*, including, of course, the Life of Fabius Maximus
- The plays of William Shakespeare
- *Leviathan* (1651) by Thomas Hobbes
- Second Treatise of Government (1689) by John Locke
- *The Wealth of Nations* (1776) by Adam Smith
- The Declaration of Independence
- The Federalist Papers
- The Constitution of the United States of America
- *Democracy in America* (1835, 1840) by Alexis de Tocqueville

This list contains only a few of the Great Books.

Here is one example from these Great Books of their wisdom. Volume II of *Democracy in America* (1840) anticipates Leviathan as identified in this book.

> Après avoir pris ainsi tour à tour dans ses puissantes mains chaque individu, et l'avoir pétri à sa guise, le souverain étend ses bras sur la société tout entière; il en couvre la surface d'un réseau de petites règles compliquées, minutieuses et uniformes, à travers lesquelles les esprits les plus originaux et les âmes les plus vigoureuses ne sauraient se faire jour pour dépasser la foule; il ne brise pas les volontés, mais il les amollit, les plie et les dirige; il force rarement d'agir, mais il s'oppose sans cesse à ce qu'on agisse; il ne détruit point, il empêche de naître; il ne tyrannise point, il gêne, il comprime, il énerve, il éteint, il hébète, et il réduit enfin chaque nation à n'être plus qu'un troupeau d'animaux timides et industrieux, dont le gouvernement est le berger. De la démocratie en Amérique, Vol. II, Part IV, Chapter VI, by Alexis de Tocqueville.

> Thus after having taken each individual one by one in His [Leviathan's] powerful hands, and having molded him to His will, the Sovereign [Leviathan] extends His arms over

the whole of Society; He covers the surface of it with a network of little complicated rules, minute and uniform, across which the most original spirits and the most vigorous souls will not be able to pass the mob; He does not break the will, He molds it, shapes it, directs it; He rarely forces action, but **He constantly opposes action**; He does not destroy, **He stops anything from being born**; He does not tyrannize, He bothers, He restrains, He enervates, He extinguishes, **He stupefies**, and He finally reduces each nation to be nothing more than **a herd of animals timid and industrious**, of which government is the Shepherd. (Emphasis and deific capitalization supplied. Author's translation.)

Fabian Libertarians will have to reteach Americans of the twenty-first century, by means of a Classical Education, what American Freedom was at the founding and will be again.

Is Freedom *as an act of will* possible, rather than *as a consequence* of social and geographic circumstances? We will have to see. We will have to try.

The End

The Fabian Libertarian *one-hundred-years plan* to restore American Freedom is thus stated. All that remains is to say to those who will join us in this noble struggle: "Be Ladies and Gentlemen. Be persistent. Practice gradualism. Have courage. Good luck." To our children and grandchildren who will glory in our successes, we offer our answer to their question: "Why do it?" Our answer:

"It is the beautiful thing to do."

Bibliography

American Psychiatric Association. *Diagnostic and Statistical Manual of Mental Disorders, 5th Edition: DSM-5*. Arlington, VA: American Psychiatric Publishing, 2013.

Aristotle. *Nicomachean Ethics*. Translated by Joe Sachs. Newburyport, MA: Focus Publishing, 2002.

Hanson, Victor Davis. Carnage and Culture: Landmark Battles in the Rise of Western Power. New York: Doubleday, 2001.

———. Fields without Dreams: Defending the Agrarian Idea. New York: The Free Press, 1996.

———. The Other Greeks: The Family Farm and the Agrarian of Western Civilization. Los Angles: University of California Press, 1999.

Hazlitt, Henry, *Economics in One Lesson*. New York: Harper & Row Publishers, 1946.

Homer. *The Iliad*. Translated by Robert Fagles. New York: Penguin Books, 1996.

Homer. *The Odyssey*. Translated by Robert Fagles. New York: Penguin Books, 1990.

Kagan, Donald. *The Peloponnesian War*. New York: Penguin Books, 2003.

Kling, Arnold. *The Three Languages of Politics*. Amazon Kindle Digital Services, LLC., 2013.

O'Rourke, P. J. Parliament of Whores: A Lone Humorist Attempts to Explain the Entire U.S. Government. New York: Grove Press, 2003.

Pease, Edward R. *The History of the Fabian Society*. New York: E. P. Dutton & Company, 1916.

Plato. *The Republic of Plato*. Translated by Allan Bloom. Second Edition. New York: Basic Books, 1991.

Plutarch. "Fabius Maximus" in *Makers of Rome.* Translated by Ian Scott-Kilvert. New York: Penguin Books, 1965.

Stout, Martha, PhD. *The Sociopath Next Door.* New York: Harmony Books, 2005.

Thucydides. *History of the Peloponnesian War.* Translated by Rex Warner. New York: Penguin Books, 1972.

Tocqueville, Alexis de. *Democracy in America.* Translated by Harvey C. Mansfield and Delba Winthrop. Chicago: University of Chicago Press, 2000.

1. The quoted sentence is found on the title page of *The History of the Fabian Society* by Edward R. Pease.
2. A common modern banality appearing in Pease's book.
3. The quotation is from *Makers of Rome: Nine Lives by Plutarch*, translated by Ian Scott-Kilvert (Penguin Books, 1965).
4. http://www.newyorker.com/magazine/2009/08/31/the-rubber-room
5. A moral community is a voluntary group of people interested a particular moral philosophy. A particular Presbyterian church is a moral community.
6. As we shall say again, people are constantly seeking to lower their costs, thereby improving the quality of their lives. One of Leviathan's main tasks is to restrain people from performing this basic life-improving function. Leviathan is inimical to life!
7. *The Sociopath Next Door* by Martha Stout, Ph.D.
8. http://climate.nasa.gov/evidence/
9. Whether any of these unethical activities actually occurred is unknowable to a layperson and no specific charge of misconduct by NASA or anyone is made in this book. There are many existing Internet stories suggesting this type of behavior. See, for example: http://jennifermarohasy.com/2008/11/correcting-ocean-cooling-nasa-changes-data-to-fit-the-models/
10. Whether any of these unethical activities actually occurred is unknowable to a layperson and no specific charge of misconduct by any pharmaceutical company or anyone is made in this book.
11. http://www.reuters.com/article/us-merck-gerberding-idUSTRE5BK2K520091221
12. http://www.morganverkamp.com/august-27-2014-press-release-statement-of-william-w-thompson-ph-d-regarding-the-2004-article-examining-the-possibility-of-a-relationship-between-mmr-vaccine-and-autism/
13. https://sharylattkisson.com/cdc-scientist-we-scheduled-meeting-to-destroy-

vaccine-autism-study-documents/
14. http://dailycaller.com/2015/02/03/obama-admin-grants-immunity-to-cdc-scientist-that-fudged-vaccine-report-whistleblower-plans-to-testify-before-congress/
15. https://www.washingtonpost.com/politics/watchdog-top-secret-service-official-wanted-information-about-chaffetz-made-public/2015/09/30/ff280378-67ae-11e5-9ef3-fde182507eac_story.html
16. http://www.washingtontimes.com/news/2013/oct/3/irs-targeted-dr-ben-carson-after-prayer-breakfast-/?page=all
17. http://www.pbs.org/newshour/bb/will-new-york-city-shut-airbnb-2/
18. http://www.bbc.com/news/world-europe-33281896
19. http://watchdog.org/238154/dc-personal-trainers-licensing/
20. http://money.cnn.com/2011/09/06/news/economy/911_compensation_fund/
21. There is a debate among psychologists and psychiatrists about the meaning of the terms antisocial personality disorder, sociopath, and psychopath. *The Diagnostic and Statistical Manual of Mental Disorders, Fifth Edition*, identifies an antisocial personality disorder. We shall not participate in the debate.
22. http://nces.ed.gov/fastfacts/display.asp?id=28
23. http://dpeaflcio.org/programs-publications/issue-fact-sheets/school-administrators-an-occupational-overview/
24. https://ballotpedia.org/Analysis_of_spending_in_America's_largest_school_districts
25. www.nps.k12.nj.us/info
26. www.d91.k12.id.us/documents/strategiplan.pdf
27. http://www.huffingtonpost.com/jack-jennings/proportion-of-us-students_b_2950948.html
28. https://en.wikipedia.org/wiki/Atlanta_Public_Schools_cheating_scandal
29. http://www.newyorker.com/magazine/2009/08/31/the-rubber-room
30. https://en.wikipedia.org/wiki/Poisoning_of_Alexander_Litvinenko
31. http://www.perseus.tufts.edu/hopper/text?doc=Perseus%3Atext%3A1999.01.0048%3Abook%3D1%3Asection%3D1344b
32. Glatt ex rel. Situtated v. Fox Searchlight Pictures, Inc., 791 F.3d 376 (2nd Cir. 2015).
33. http://www.politifact.com/truth-o-meter/statements/2015/jul/13/bernie-s/bernie-sanders-says-real-unemployment-rate-african/
34. In general, the prices of commodities and services trend down because of productivity increases.
35. One should never violate the law. Price comparisons with non-American

36. https://masshealthdruglist.ehs.state.ma.us/MHDL/pubtheradetail.do?id=213
37. One should never violate the law. Using pet medicine for people violates the law. Ordering penicillin from Mexico for import into America violates the law. These facts are recited simply to show that the cost in Massachusetts of $200 for a penicillin injection is probably 40 times the free market price.
38. The Community Reinvestment Act (CRA) of 1977
39. https://www.ssa.gov/oact/progdata/fundFAQ.html
40. http://fee.org/freeman/the-myth-of-the-social-security-trust-fund/
41. In *The Matrix*, our hero Neo must take the Red Pill, rather than the Blue Pill, in order to be able to see the world as it really is.
42. Talk about "Clean Water Theater", the people of Flint, Michigan, have been drinking lead-laced Government-provided tap water for the year preceding this writing. In August, 2015, the EPA was involved in a toxic spill into the Animas River, Colorado, turning the once beautiful river into a golden and poisonous sludge.
43. "Weird" simply means that there is no accounting for taste. Each of us appears "weird" to others in some respect, especially cross-culturally. A **radical tolerance** for human differences is what distinguishes Libertarians from Progressives and Conservatives.
44. http://www.nature.com/nature/journal/v529/n7586/full/nature16477.html
45. William Shakespeare, *Julius Caesar*, Act 3, Scene 1, line 273
46. James Robert Clapper, Jr., the current Director of National Intelligence testified on March 12, 2013, in response to the question of Oregon Democrat Senator Ron Wyden: "Does the NSA collect any type of data at all on millions or hundreds of millions of Americans?" Clapper: "No, sir." Senator Wyden: "It does not?" Clapper: "Not wittingly. There are cases where they could inadvertently, perhaps, collect, but not wittingly." Edward Snowden, a former Central Intelligence Agency (CIA) employee, has suggested otherwise.
47. Aristotle's *Nicomachean Ethics*, 1123b32.
48. *Ibid.*, 1134a26-28.
49. https://www.cals.ncsu.edu/CollegeRelations/AGRICU.htm
50. https://nsa.gov1.info/data/index.html
51. The pervert might defend his intrusion by claiming to be looking after your safety by examining you for venereal disease. The odds of the pervert finding evidence of venereal disease on your genitalia are higher than NSA discovering evidence of your terrorist intentions in your intercepted telephone calls.

52   https://nsa.gov1.info/utah-data-center/
53   https://theintercept.com/2015/07/30/jimmy-carter-u-s-oligarchy-unlimited-political-bribery/
54   https://en.wikipedia.org/wiki/Terri_Schiavo_case
55   http://www.gallup.com/poll/154799/americans-including-catholics-say-birth-control-morally.aspx
56   Other questions at the margins of property include the rights of children and the rights of animals. First secure the core of property rights. Then, worry about the margins.
57   For the purposes of this argument, this proposed abortion is assumed to be legal. Beauty is in the perception. Obviously, a different moral problem is presented if this decision is made at one week after fertilization.
58   https://en.wikipedia.org/wiki/Libertarian_Republican
59   http://www.nytimes.com/2016/01/06/upshot/why-the-Government-owns-so-much-land-in-the-west.html
60   http://www.encyclopedia.com/doc/1G2-3401804525.html

Index

A

abortion, 13, 141–48, 152–53
    ethics of, 147, 149
    morality of, 147, 149
    politics of, 147, 149
abortion debate, 142–44, 146–47
Airbnb.com, 16, 46, 114, 121, 160
Alcibiades, 90
American Association of Retired Persons (AARP), 43
American Freedom, xvii–xx, 69, 86, 101–4, 121, 123, 142, 155, 157–60, 164
    restoration of, 81, 104, 123
anthropomorphization, 144–46
appetite for honor, 82, 88, 93
Aristotle, 15, 33, 82, 87–91, 147, 149, 163, 165
Aristotle's politics, 15, 111
artificial intelligence (AI), 5
atonement, 144

B

bankruptcy, 53–55, 134, 156–57
barbarism, 61, 63
Battle of Cannae, xvi–xvii
Becket, Thomas, 9, 13–14, 31

biosphere, 135–37, 139–40

C

Carnegie, Andrew, 86–87
Carthaginians, 81, 107–8
Casilinum, 107–8
Centers for Disease Control and prevention (CDC), 10, 23, 43, 72, 77, 129
Central Intelligence Agency (CIA), 122, 131, 169
Civil War, 130–31
Classical Education, 18, 162, 164
Clayton County Department, 95
Common Core, 56
Community Reinvestment Act (CRA), 155, 169
compact fluorescent light (CFL), 18, 69
competition, 16, 45, 96, 115, 160
conscience, 8, 11–14, 21–22, 30–31, 91, 141
Conservatives, 60–64, 66, 68, 141, 169
Constitution, xviii, 76, 128–29, 163
courage, xviii, 2, 82–83, 92–93, 164

D

debt, 13, 30, 53–55, 91, 156

Declaration of War, 130–32
Deep Plowing, 70–71, 78
democracy, 15, 68, 76, 105, 111, 159, 163, 166
Democratic Totalitarianism, xix, 20, 62, 64, 69–70, 74, 158
depression, 34, 52–53, 155
de Tocqueville, Alexis, 163
doctoring, 51
drugs, 9, 13, 41, 61–62, 66, 126, 128, 169

E

economics, 33, 43, 58, 113–14, 155, 165
   simple rules of, 34–35
economy, 16, 56, 59, 156, 160, 162
   free, 50
Edison, Thomas, 4–5, 18
education, 20, 23, 25, 101–2, 112–13, 120, 162
   board of, 102–3
   nongovernment, 25
   public, 2, 21, 56, 102–3
   secondary, 61
education taxes, 24
Education Theater, 23, 25, 29
employment, 13, 27, 35, 41–42, 67, 114–15, 118, 125
   lifetime, 18
   nongovernment, 26–27
   of sociopaths, 8, 12
   total cost of, 40–41
Enlightenment, xix, 91
Ennius, 107
Environmental Protection Agency (EPA), 129, 139, 169
Escalante, Jaime, 29
ethics, 101, 136, 147–48
exaggeration, 89

F

Fabian Libertarianism, xiii, xix, 83
Fabian Libertarian Plan, 103–4, 106, 108, 123
Fabian Libertarians, 17, 59, 69, 71, 83, 86–87, 89–91, 93–94, 96, 100–106, 108, 110, 112–13, 117, 122, 139, 142, 153–55, 157, 161, 164
Fabius Maximus, xiii, xvi–xvii, xix, 80, 94, 106–8, 163, 166
Federal Aviation Administration (FAA), 73
Federal Government, 15, 43, 105, 126, 128–30, 132, 156
Fellowship of Reason (FOR), 1, 4
Food and Drug Administration (FDA), 43, 129
freedom, xviii–xx, 7, 16, 31, 35, 38, 64, 76, 79, 81, 87, 100, 104, 118, 121, 124, 135, 140, 142, 157–59, 161–62, 164
   definition of, xviii, 133
   of employment, 35
   invention of, 157, 159
free-market economy, 40, 42, 44, 47–48, 50–51
friendliness, 2, 82, 90, 93

G

Gates, Bill, 65–66, 86–87
General Electric (GE), 1–2, 5–6, 18
General Will, xix, 21, 31, 64, 69, 74, 119, 121
generosity, 2, 82, 85–86, 88, 93

gentleness, 82, 88–89, 93
Georgia Election Code, 100
Georgia Libertarian Party, xviii, 81
government
  legitimate functions of, 15, 43, 57–58, 104, 126, 132
  totalitarian, 70, 87, 157
Government Education, 18, 20–21, 23, 102, 112
government monopoly, 27, 47, 119, 122
Great Depression II, 155–57
Great Leap Forward, 70, 78
Great Pacific garbage patch, 134
Greece, ancient, xviii, 91–92, 126, 129, 158, 161–62

H

Hannibal, xiii, xvi, 80–81, 106–8
happiness, pursuit of, xviii, 75–76, 79, 124, 133, 148
Health and Human Services (HHS), 43
healthcare, 34, 38, 42–44, 49–51, 120
healthcare insurance, 38, 40, 43–45, 48, 51
High School Proficiency Assessment (HSPA), 24
historical determinism, 92
human resources (HR), 12, 14, 25, 155

I

IBM Selectric typewriters, 113–14
independence, xviii–xix, 2, 75, 92, 151
information filters, 8, 23, 25
Innocents, 26
innovators, 26, 28–29, 31

Internal Revenue Service (IRS), 14, 132
Internet, 30, 39, 47, 73, 115

J

justice, 2, 74, 82, 89, 91, 93, 126, 128

K

Kling, Arnold, 60–61

L

Leviathan
  benefit of, 55, 59
  constituencies of, 43, 48
  employees of, 26, 28
  Leviathan Big Government, 16–17, 38, 42–44, 46, 51–56, 58, 60–61, 67, 97, 119, 121, 125–26, 141–42, 155–57, 160
  absence of, 120–22
Leviathan Education, 19, 22–26, 28–29, 31–32, 58, 60, 89
Leviathan Healthcare Insurance, 42, 45, 47, 49, 58
Leviathan Mainstream Media, 11, 18, 58
Libertarianism, xiii, 72, 126, 133
Libertarian Party, xviii, 109, 154, 156
Locke, John, xix
Luddite Fallacy, 113–14, 116, 160
Luddites, 40, 113, 115
Lysenko, Trofim, 70–71

M

Madame Curie, 65–66

magnanimity, 2, 82, 87–88, 93
magnificence, 2, 82, 86, 88, 93
Mao Zedong, 69–71
Metropolitan Statistical Area (MSA), 58, 128
military, 126, 129, 131–32
monopoly, 15, 25, 29, 51
morality, 2, 5, 7, 148–49

N

National Education Association (NEA), 1–2, 5–6
National Institutes of Health (NIH), 43
National Ocean and Atmospheric Administration (NOAA), 9
natural law, 70, 74, 78
Nepos, Gaius Flaminius, 80

O

Obamacare, 38, 43, 49–50, 53, 56
oligarchy, 15, 56, 111, 124

P

Peloponnesian War, 90, 163, 165–66
penicillin, 47, 169
Planned Parenthood Federation of America, 13
Plato, 57, 163, 165
Plutarch, xvi, 80, 163, 166–67
power plants, coal-fired, 136–37
pride, xx, 2–3, 7, 65, 67, 82, 86–87
privacy, 70, 73–74, 79, 117, 119
    zone of, 70, 76–79

productivity, xviii, 2, 36, 40, 65, 67, 86, 92, 117, 119, 160
profits, 9, 30, 36, 114–15
Progressives, 61–64, 66, 68, 169
pro-life, 147, 153
pro-life position, 144–45
propaganda, 6, 14, 25, 55
property rights, xviii–xix, 44, 51, 64, 74–76, 79, 87, 133, 161
    core of, 153, 170
    private, 121, 140
    protection of, xviii, xx, 87, 142

R

recessions, 52–53
responsibility, 62, 124, 135, 140
righteous indignation, 2, 82, 91, 93
Rousseau, Jean-Jacques, xix, 20–21, 31, 64, 69, 74, 119, 121, 125, 158
Russell, Bertrand, 141–42

S

Savin word processors, 113–14
science, dictatorship of, 69, 71, 78
Scientism, 69, 71
Second Punic War, xvi, xix, 106–7
Shaw, Bernard, xiii–xiv
slavery, xv, 158–59
Slugs, 26, 29–30, 93
Smith, Adam, xix, 13, 30, 75, 91
Socialists, xiv–xv, xvii, 69, 125, 160, 162
Social Security, 40, 42, 55, 67, 156
sociopaths, 8–9, 11–12, 21–22, 26, 30–31, 35, 94, 142
    competent, 11–13, 22, 30

Socrates, 89
Stars, 26–28, 31
superorganisms, 1, 4–18, 22, 31, 53–54, 57, 139
  sociopathic, 26, 35, 57–58

T

taxation, 63, 126, 132–33
teaching, 22, 28, 89, 162
temperance, 82, 85, 93
Time Markers, 26
truthfulness, 2, 82, 89, 93

U

Uber, 7, 16, 46, 114, 121
unemployment, xiv, 38, 41, 61, 66

V

vaccines, 44, 120

W

wages, xiv–xv, 35–36, 38, 40–41, 86
  federal minimum, 37–38
water, 12, 34, 62, 64, 66, 75, 92, 102, 120, 133–34, 137
Webb, Sidney, xiv
whistle-blowers, 14, 27

Y

yeoman farmers, xvii–xviii, 5–6, 91–92, 126, 129, 158–62

Printed in the United States
By Bookmasters